WANTED

The World's Most Sought After Fugitives

WANTED

The World's Most Sought After Fugitives

Platinum Press Inc.

New York

Copyright © 2002 by Platinum Press Inc.

Library of Congress Cataloging in Publication data has been applied for

ISBN 1-879582-60-0

Designed and edited by Glenn Gottlieb

Printed and bound in the United States of America

Platinum Press Inc.
311 Crossways Park Drive
Woodbury, N.Y. 11797

USA

2002

1 2 3 4 5 6 7 8 9

TABLE OF CONTENTS

INTRODUCTION

WANTED
The World's Most Sought-After Fugitives

This book contains complete descriptions and photos of the most wanted criminals and terrorists in the world. It is not confined to fugitives sought only by the FBI, but also men and women on the run from many other law enforcement agencies. Included in the U.S. Government Agencies are The Drug Enforcement Administration, Bureau of Alcohol, Tobacco & Firearms, U.S. Secret Service, Department of State, U.S. Customs Service, Marshals Service, Postal Service, the Criminal Investigative Services of the various Armed Forces, and many, many more.

Additionally, we have included fugitives wanted by many state and municipal police departments, as well as some private organizations such as Wells Fargo, Bail Jumpers, and numerous Bounty Hunter organizations. There are also individuals wanted by the Royal Canadian Mounted Police. Since the great majority of these fugitives have rewards offered for information leading to their arrest, readers of this book have an opportunity to earn substantial sums of money if they aid in locating any of these individuals. **Caution: Do not attempt to apprehend any of these individuals. If you have information concerning a fugitive, please contact the appropriate law enforcement agency. A list of phone numbers, addresses and web sites is included in the back of this book.**

Also contained within these pages is fascinating historical data on the FBI as well as valuable reference information, including The U. S. Department of Justice's REWARDS FOR JUSTICE PROGRAM, and contact data for various government and private law enforcement organizations.

Good Hunting!!

FIDELITY BRAVERY AND INTEGRITY

★ ★ ★ ★ ★

A History of the FBI

From its controversial beginnings and the development of the Most Wanted program, through the depression and times of war, to its emergence as the world's preeminent crime fighting organization, we present the colorful history of the Federal Bureau of Investigation.

ORIGINS (1908 – 1910)

The FBI originated from a force of Special Agents created in 1908 by Attorney General Charles Bonaparte during the Presidency of Theodore Roosevelt. The two men first met when they both spoke at a meeting of the Baltimore Civil Service Reform Association. Roosevelt, then Civil Service Commissioner, boasted of his reforms in federal law enforcement. It was 1892, a time when law enforcement was often political rather than professional. Roosevelt spoke with pride of his insistence that Border Patrol applicants pass marksmanship tests, with the most accurate getting the jobs. Following Roosevelt on the program, Bonaparte countered, tongue in cheek, that target shooting was not the way to get the best men. "Roosevelt should have had the men shoot at each other, and given the jobs to the survivors."

Roosevelt and Bonaparte both were "Progressives." They shared the conviction that efficiency and expertise, not political connections, should determine who could best serve in government. Theodore Roosevelt became President of the United States in 1901; four years later, he appointed Bonaparte to be Attorney General. In 1908, Bonaparte applied that Progressive philosophy to the Department of Justice by creating a corps of Special Agents. It had neither a name nor an officially designated leader other than the Attorney General. Yet, these former detectives and Secret Service men were the forerunners of the FBI.

Today, most Americans take for granted that our country needs a federal investigative service, but in 1908, the establishment of this kind of agency at a national level was highly controversial. The U.S. Constitution is based on "federalism:" a national government with jurisdiction over matters that crossed boundaries, like interstate commerce and foreign affairs, with all other powers reserved to the states. Through the 1800s, Americans usually looked to cities, counties, and states to fulfill most government responsibilities. However, by the 20th century, easier transportation and communications had created a climate of opinion favorable to the federal government establishing a strong investigative tradition.

The impulse among the American people toward a responsive federal government, coupled with an idealistic, reformist spirit, characterized what is known as the Progressive Era, from approximately 1900 to 1918. The Progressive generation believed that government intervention was necessary to produce justice in an industrial society. Moreover, it looked to "experts" in all phases of industry and government to produce that just society.

President Roosevelt personified Progressivism at the national level. A federal investigative force consisting of well-disciplined experts and designed to fight corruption and crime fit Roosevelt's Progressive scheme of government. Attorney General Bonaparte shared his President's Progressive philosophy. However, the Department of Justice under Bonaparte had no investigators of its own except for a few Special Agents who carried out specific assignments for the Attorney General, and a force of Examiners (trained as accountants) who reviewed the financial transactions of the federal courts. Since its beginning in 1870, the Department of Justice used funds appropriated to investigate federal crimes to hire private detectives first, and later investigators from other federal agencies. (Federal crimes are those that were considered interstate or occurred on federal government reservations.)

By 1907, the Department of Justice most frequently called upon Secret Service "operatives" to conduct investigations. These men were well-trained, dedicated -- and expensive. Moreover, they reported not to the Attorney General, but to the Chief of the Secret Service. This situation frustrated Bonaparte, who wanted complete control of investigations under his jurisdiction. Congress provided the impetus for Bonaparte to acquire his own force. On May 27, 1908, it enacted a law preventing the Department of Justice from engaging Secret Service operatives.

The following month, Attorney General Bonaparte appointed a force of Special Agents within the Department of Justice. Accordingly, ten former Secret Service employees and a number of Department of Justice peonage (i.e., compulsory servitude) investigators became Special Agents of the Department of Justice. On July 26, 1908, Bonaparte ordered them to report to Chief Examiner Stanley W. Finch. This action is celebrated as the beginning of the FBI.

Both Attorney General Bonaparte and President Theodore Roosevelt, who completed their terms in March 1909, recommended that the force of 34 Agents become a permanent part of the Department of Justice. Attorney General George Wickersham, Bonaparte's successor, named the force the Bureau of Investigation on March 16, 1909. At that time, the title of Chief Examiner was changed to Chief of the Bureau of Investigation. ★

EARLY DAYS (1910 – 1921)

When the Bureau was established, there were few federal crimes. The Bureau of Investigation primarily investigated violations of laws involving national banking, bankruptcy, naturalization, antitrust, peonage, and land fraud. Because the early Bureau provided no formal training, previous law enforcement experience or a background in the law was considered desirable.

The first major expansion in Bureau jurisdiction came in June 1910 when the Mann ("White Slave") Act was passed, making it a crime to transport women over state lines for immoral purposes. It also provided a tool by which the federal government could investigate criminals who evaded state laws but had no other federal violations. Finch became Commissioner of White Slavery Act violations in

A. Bruce Bielaski

1912, and former Special Examiner A. Bruce Bielaski became the new Bureau of Investigation Chief.

Over the next few years, the number of Special Agents grew to more than 300, and these individuals were complemented by another 300 Support Employees. Field offices existed from the Bureau's inception. Each field operation was controlled by a Special Agent in Charge who was responsible to Washington. Most field offices were located in major cities. However, several were located near the Mexican border where they concentrated on smuggling, neutrality violations, and intelligence collec-

The Bureau in the early days

tion, often in connection with the Mexican revolution.

With the April 1917 entry of the United States into World War I during Woodrow Wilson's administration, the Bureau's work was increased again. As a result of the war, the Bureau acquired responsibility for the Espionage, Selective Service, and Sabotage Acts, and assisted the Department of Labor by investigating enemy aliens. During these years Special Agents with general investigative experience and facility in certain languages augmented the Bureau.

William J. Flynn, former head of the Secret Service, became Director of the Bureau of Investigation in July 1919 and was the first to use that title. In October 1919, passage of the National Motor Vehicle Theft Act gave the Bureau of Investigation another tool by which to prosecute criminals who previously evaded the law by crossing state lines. With the return of the country to "nor-

William J. Flynn

malcy" under President Warren G. Harding in 1921, the Bureau of Investigation returned to its pre-war role of fighting the few federal crimes. ★

THE LAWLESS YEARS
(1921 – 1933)

The years from 1921 to 1933 were sometimes called the "lawless years" because of gangsterism and the public disregard for Prohibition, which made it illegal to sell or import intoxicating beverages. Prohibition created a new federal medium for fighting crime, but the Department of the Treasury, not the Department of Justice, had jurisdiction for these violations.

Attacking crimes that were federal in scope but local in jurisdiction called for creative solutions. The Bureau of Investigation had limited success using its narrow jurisdiction to investigate some of the criminals of "the gangster era." For example, it investigated Al Capone as a "fugitive federal witness." Federal investigation of a resurgent white supremacy movement also required creativity. The Ku Klux Klan (KKK), dormant since the late 1800s, was revived in part to counteract the economic gains made by African Americans during World War I. The Bureau of Investigation used the Mann Act to bring Louisiana's philandering KKK "Imperial Kleagle" to justice.

Through these investigations and through more traditional investigations of neutrality violations and

William J. Burns

antitrust violations, the Bureau of Investigation gained stature. Although the Harding Administration suffered from unqualified and sometimes corrupt officials, the Progressive Era reform tradition continued among the professional Department of Justice Special Agents. The new Bureau of Investigation Director, William J. Burns, who had previously run his own detective agency, appointed 26-year-old J. Edgar Hoover as Assistant Director. Hoover, a graduate of George Washington University Law School, had worked for the Department of Justice since 1917, where he headed the enemy alien operations during

World War I and assisted in the General Intelligence Division under Attorney General A. Mitchell Palmer, investigating suspected anarchists and communists.

After Harding died in 1923, his successor, Calvin Coolidge, appointed replacements for Harding's cronies in the Cabinet. For the new Attorney General, Coolidge appointed attorney Harlan Fiske Stone. Stone then, on May 10, 1924, selected Hoover to head the

J. Edgar Hoover

Bureau of Investigation. By inclination and training, Hoover embodied the Progressive tradition. His appointment ensured that the Bureau of Investigation would keep that tradition alive.

When Hoover took over, the Bureau of Investigation had approximately 650 employees, including 441 Special Agents who worked in field offices in nine cities. By the end of the decade, there

FBI Headquarters

were approximately 30 field offices, with Divisional headquarters in New York, Baltimore, Atlanta, Cincinnati, Chicago, Kansas City, San Antonio, San Francisco, and Portland. He immediately fired those Agents he considered unqualified and proceeded to professionalize the organization. For example, Hoover abolished the seniority rule of promotion and introduced uniform performance appraisals. At the beginning of the decade, the Bureau of Investigation established field offices in nine cities. He also scheduled regular inspections of the operations in all field offices. Then, in January 1928, Hoover established a formal training course for new Agents, including the requirement that New Agents had to be in the 25-35 year range to apply. He also returned to the earlier preference for Special Agents with law or accounting experience.

The new Director was also keenly aware that the Bureau of Investigation could not fight crime without public support. In remarks prepared for the Attorney General in 1925, he wrote, "The Agents of the Bureau of Investigation have been impressed with the fact that the real problem of law enforcement is in trying to obtain the cooperation and sympathy of the public and that they cannot hope to get such cooperation until they themselves merit the respect of the public." Also in 1925, Agent Edwin C. Shanahan became the first Agent to be killed in the line of duty when he was murdered by a car thief.

In the early days of Hoover's directorship, a long held goal of American law enforcement was achieved: the establishment of an Identification Division. Tracking criminals by means of identification records had been considered a crucial tool of law enforcement since the 19th century, and matching fingerprints was considered the most accurate method. By 1922, many large cities had started their own fingerprint collections.

In keeping with the Progressive Era tradition of federal assistance to localities, the Department of Justice created a Bureau of Criminal Identification in 1905 in order to provide a centralized reference collection of fingerprint cards. In 1907, the collection was moved, as a money-saving measure, to Leavenworth Federal Penitentiary, where it was staffed by convicts. Understandably suspicious of this arrangement, police departments formed their own centralized identification bureau maintained by the International Association of Chiefs of Police. It refused to share its data with the Bureau of Criminal Investigation. In 1924, Congress was persuaded to merge the two collections in Washington, D.C., under Bureau of Investigation administration. As a result, law enforcement agencies across the country began contributing fingerprint cards to the Bureau of Investigation by 1926.

By the end of the decade, Special Agent training was institutionalized, the field office inspection system was solidly in place, and the National Division of Identification and Information was collecting and compiling uniform crime statistics for the entire United States. In addition, studies were underway that would lead to the creation of the Technical Laboratory and Uniform Crime Reports. The Bureau was equipped to end the "lawless years." ★

Edwin C. Shanahan

In 1907, the centralized reference collection of fingerprint cards was moved to Leavenworth Federal Penitentiary, where it was staffed by convicts. Understandably suspicious of this arrangement, police departments formed their own centralized identification bureau.

THE NEW DEAL
(1933 – late 1930s)

The 1929 stock market crash and the Great Depression brought hard times to America. Hard times, in turn, created more criminals – and also led Americans to escape their troubles through newspapers, radio, and movies.

To combat the crime wave, President Franklin D. Roosevelt influenced Congress in his first administration to expand federal jurisdiction, and his Attorney General, Homer Cummings, fought an unrelenting campaign against rampant crime. One case highlighting the rampant crime included the swindling and murder of members of the Osage Indian tribe in Oklahoma for the rights to their oil fields.

The FBI investigated murder in the Osage oil fields

Noting the widespread interest of the media in this war against crime, Hoover carried the message of FBI work through them to the American people. For example, in 1932, the first issue of the FBI Law Enforcement Bulletin - then called Fugitives Wanted by Police, was published. Hoover became as adept at publicizing his agency's work as he was at administering it. Prior to 1933, Bureau Agents had developed an esprit de corps, but the public considered them interchangeable with other federal investigators. Three years later, mere identification with the FBI was a source of special pride to its employees and commanded instant recognition and respect from the public. By the end of the decade, the Bureau had field offices in 42 cities and employed 654 Special Agents and 1141 Support Employees.

During the early and mid-1930s several crucial decisions solidified the Bureau's position as the nation's premier law enforcement agency. Responding to the kidnapping of the Lindbergh baby, in 1932, Congress passed a federal kidnapping statute. Then in May and June 1934, with gangsters like John Dillinger evading capture by crossing over state lines, it passed a number of federal crime laws that significantly enhanced the Bureau's jurisdiction. In the wake of the Kansas City Massacre, Congress also gave Bureau Agents statutory authority to carry guns and make arrests.

The Bureau of Investigation was renamed the United States Bureau of Investigation on July 1, 1932. Then, beginning July 1, 1933, the Department of Justice experimented for almost two years with a

CHAS. A. LINDBERGH, JR.
OF HOPEWELL, N. J.
SON OF COL. CHAS. A. LINDBERGH
World-Famous Aviator

This child was kidnaped from his home in Hopewell, N. J., between 8 and 10 p. m. on Tuesday, March 1, 1932.

DESCRIPTION:

Age, 20 months   Hair, blond, curly
Weight, 27 to 30 lbs.   Eyes, dark blue
Height, 29 inches   Complexion, light
Deep dimple in center of chin
Dressed in one-piece coverall night suit

ADDRESS ALL COMMUNICATIONS TO
COL. H. N. SCHWARZKOPF, TRENTON, N. J., or
COL. CHAS. A. LINDBERGH, HOPEWELL, N. J.

ALL COMMUNICATIONS WILL BE TREATED IN CONFIDENCE

March 11, 1932
COL. H. NORMAN SCHWARZKOPF
Supt. New Jersey State Police, Trenton, N. J.

This Wanted poster was issued after the kidnapping of the Lindbergh baby

The Kansas City Massacre

The Department of Justice

Division of Investigation that included the Bureau of Prohibition. Public confusion between Bureau of Investigation Special Agents and Prohibition Agents led to a permanent name change in 1935 for the agency composed of Department of Justice's investigators: the Federal Bureau of Investigation was thus born.

Contributing to its forensic expertise, the Bureau established its Technical Laboratory in 1932. Journalist Rex Collier called it "a novel research laboratory where government criminologists will match wits with underworld cunning." Originally the small laboratory operated strictly as a research facility. However, it benefitted from expanded federal funding, eventually housing specialized microscopes and extensive reference collections of guns, watermarks, typefaces, and automobile tire designs.

In 1935, the FBI National Academy was established to train police officers in modern investigative meth-

ods, since at that time only a few states and localities provided formal training to their peace officers. The National Academy (pictured left and below) taught investigative techniques to police officials throughout the United States, and starting in the 1940s, from all over the world.

The legal tools given to the FBI by Congress, as well as Bureau initiatives to upgrade its own professionalism and that of law enforcement, resulted in the arrest or demise of all the major gangsters by 1936. By that time, however, Fascism in Adolph Hitler's Germany and Benito Mussolini's Italy, and Communism in Josef Stalin's Soviet Union threatened American democratic principles. With war on the horizon, a new set of challenges faced the FBI. ★

Officers in the National Academy

Class in session at the National Academy

WORLD WAR II PERIOD
(late 1930s – 1945)

Germany, Italy, and Japan embarked on an unchecked series of invasions during the late 1930s. Hitler and Mussolini supported the Spanish Falangists in their successful civil war against the "Loyalist" Spanish government (1937-39). Although many Europeans and North Americans considered the Spanish Civil War an opportunity to destroy Fascism, the United States, Great Britain, and France remained neutral; only Russia supported the Loyalists. To the shock of those who admired Russia for its active opposition to Fascism, Stalin and Hitler signed a nonaggression pact in August 1939. The following month Germany and Soviet Russia seized Poland. A short time later, Russia overran the Baltic States. Finland, while maintaining its independence, lost western Karelia to Russia. Great Britain and France declared war on Germany, which formed the "Axis" with Japan and Italy--and World War II began. The United States, however, continued to adhere to the neutrality acts it had passed in the mid-1930s.

As these events unfolded in Europe, the American Depression continued. The Depression provided as fertile an environment for radicalism in the United States as it did in Europe. European Fascists had their counterparts and supporters in the United States in the German-American Bund, the Silver Shirts, and similar groups. At the same time, labor unrest, racial disturbances, and sympathy for the Spanish Loyalists presented an unparalleled opportunity for the American Communist Party to gain adherents. The FBI was alert to these Fascist and Communist groups as threats to American security.

Authority to investigate these organizations came in 1936 with President Roosevelt's authorization through Secretary of State Cordell Hull. A 1939 Presidential Directive further strengthened the FBI's authority to investigate subversives in the United States, and Congress reinforced it by passing the Smith Act in 1940, outlawing advocacy of violent overthrow of the government.

With the actual outbreak of war in 1939, the responsibilities of the FBI escalated. Subversion, sabotage, and espionage became major concerns. In addition to Agents trained in general intelligence work, at least one Agent trained in defense plant protection was placed in each of the FBI's 42 field offices. The FBI also developed a network of informational sources, often using members of fraternal or veterans' organizations. With leads developed by these intelligence networks and through their own work, Special Agents investigated potential threats to national security.

Great Britain stood virtually alone against the Axis powers after France fell to the Germans in 1940. An Axis victory in Europe and Asia would threaten democracy in North America. Because of the Nazi-Soviet Pact, the American Communist Party and its sympathizers posed a double-edged threat to American interests. Under the direction of Russia, the American Communist Party vigorously advocated continued neutrality for the United States.

In 1940 and 1941, the United States moved further and further away from neutrality, actively aiding the Allies. In late 1940, Congress reestablished the draft. The FBI was responsible for locating draft evaders and deserters.

Without warning, the Germans attacked Russia on June 22, 1941. Thereafter, the FBI focused its internal security efforts on potentially dangerous German, Italian, and Japanese nationals as well as native-born Americans whose beliefs and activities aided the Axis powers.

The FBI also participated in intelligence collection. Here the Technical Laboratory played a pioneering role. Its highly skilled and inventive staff cooperated with engineers, scientists, and cryptographers in other agencies to enable the United States to penetrate and sometimes control the flow of information from the belligerents in the Western Hemisphere.

Sabotage investigations were another FBI responsibility. In June 1942, a major, yet unsuccessful, attempt at sabotage was made on American soil. Two German submarines let off four saboteurs each at Amagansett, Long Island, and Ponte Vedra Beach, Florida. These men had been trained by Germany in explosives, chemistry, secret writing, and how to blend into American surroundings. While still in German clothes, the New York group encountered a Coast Guard sentinel patrolling the beach, who ultimately allowed them to pass. However, afraid of capture, saboteur George Dasch turned himself in--and assisted the FBI in locating and arresting the rest of the team. The swift capture of these Nazi saboteurs helped to allay fear of Axis subversion and bolstered Americans' faith in the FBI.

Also, before U.S. entry into the War, the FBI uncovered another major espionage ring. This group, the Frederick Duquesne spy ring, was the largest one discovered up to that time. The FBI was assisted by a loyal American with German relatives who acted as a double agent. For nearly two years the FBI ran a radio station for him, learning what Germany was sending to its spies in the United States while controlling the information that was being transmitted to Germany. The investigation led to the arrest and conviction of 33 spies.

War for the United States began December 7, 1941, when Japanese armed forces attacked ships and facilities at Pearl Harbor, Hawaii. The United States immediately declared war on Japan, and the next day Germany and Italy declared war on the United States. By 9:30 p.m., Eastern Standard Time, on December 7, the FBI was in a wartime mode. FBI Headquarters and the 54 field offices were placed on 24-hour schedules. On December 7 and 8, the FBI arrested previously identified aliens who threatened national security and turned them over to military or immigration authorities.

A World War II internment camp

At this time, the FBI augmented its Agent force with National Academy graduates, who took an abbreviated training course. As a result, the total number of FBI employees rose from 7,400 to over 13,000, including approximately 4,000 Agents, by the end of 1943.

Traditional war-related investigations did not occupy all the FBI's time. For example, the Bureau continued to carry out civil rights investigations. Segregation, which was legal at the time, was the rule in the Armed Services and in virtually the entire defense industry in the 1940s. Under pressure from African-American organizations, the President appointed a Fair Employment Practices Commission (FEPC). The FEPC had no enforcement authority. However, the FBI could arrest individuals who impeded the war effort. The Bureau assisted the FEPC when a Philadelphia transit workers' union went out on strike against an FEPC desegregation order. The strike ended when it appeared that the FBI was about to arrest its leaders.

The most serious discrimination during World War II was the decision to evacuate Japanese nationals and American citizens of Japanese descent from the West Coast and send them to internment camps. Because the FBI had arrested the individuals whom it considered security threats, FBI Director Hoover took the position that confining others was unnecessary. The President and Attorney General, however, chose to support the military assessment that evacuation and internment were imperative. Ultimately, the FBI became responsible for arresting curfew and evacuation violators.

While most FBI personnel during the war worked traditional war-related or criminal cases, one contingent of Agents was unique. Separated from Bureau rolls, these Agents, with the help of FBI Legal Attaches, composed the Special Intelligence Service (SIS) in Latin America. Established by President Roosevelt in 1940, the SIS was to provide information on Axis activities in South America and to destroy its intelligence and propaganda networks. Several hundred thousand Germans or German descendants and numerous Japanese lived in South America. They provided pro-Axis pressure and cover for Axis communications facilities. Nevertheless, in every South American country, the SIS was instrumental in bringing about a situation in which, by 1944, continued support for the Nazis became intolerable or impractical.

Non-war acts were not limited to civil rights cases. In 1940, the FBI Disaster Squad was created when the FBI Identification Division was called upon to identify some Bureau employees who were on a flight which had crashed near Lovettsville, Virginia.

In April 1945, President Roosevelt died, and Vice President Harry Truman took office as President. Before the end of the month, Hitler committed suicide and the German commander in Italy surrendered. Although the May 1945 surrender of Germany ended the war in Europe, war continued in the Pacific until August 14, 1945.

The world that the FBI faced in September 1945 was very different from the world of 1939 when the war began. American isolationism had effectively ended, and, economically, the United States had become the world's most powerful nation. At home, organized labor had achieved a strong foothold; African Americans and women, having tasted equality during wartime labor shortages, had developed aspirations and the means of achieving the goals that these groups had lacked before the war. The American Communist Party possessed an unparalleled confidence, while overseas the Soviet Union strengthened its grasp on the countries it had wrested from German occupation-making it plain that its plans to expand Communist influence had not abated. And hanging over the euphoria of a world once more at peace was the mushroom cloud of atomic weaponry. ★

POSTWAR AMERICA
(1945 – 1960s)

In February 1946 Stalin gave a public address in which he implied that future wars were inevitable until Communism replaced capitalism worldwide. Events in Europe and North America convinced Congress that Stalin was well on his way to achieving his goal. The Russian veto prevented the United Nations from curbing Soviet expansion under its auspices.

Americans feared Communist expansion was not limited to Europe. By 1947, ample evidence existed that pro-Soviet individuals had infiltrated the American Government. In June, 1945, the FBI raided the offices of Amerasia, a magazine concerned with the Far East, and discovered a large number of classified State Department documents. Several months later the Canadians arrested 22 people for trying to steal atomic secrets. Previously, Americans felt secure behind their monopoly of the atomic bomb. Fear of a Russian bomb now came to dominate American thinking. The Soviets detonated their own bomb in 1949.

Counteracting the Communist threat became a paramount focus of government at all levels, as well as the private sector. While U.S. foreign policy concentrated on defeating Communist expansion abroad, many U.S. citizens sought to defeat the Communist threat at home. The American Communist Party worked through front organizations or influenced other Americans who agreed with their current propaganda ("fellow travelers").

Since 1917, the FBI and its predecessor agencies had investigated suspected acts of espionage and sabotage. In 1939 and again in 1943, Presidential directives had authorized the FBI to carry out investigations of threats to national security. This role was clarified and expanded under Presidents Truman and Dwight D. Eisenhower. Any public or private agency or individual with information about subversive activities was urged to report it to the FBI. A poster to that effect was distributed to police departments throughout the country. At the same time, it warned Americans to "avoid reporting malicious gossip or idle rumors." The FBI's authority to conduct background investigations on present and prospective government employees also expanded dramatically in the postwar years. The 1946 Atomic Energy Act gave the FBI "responsibility for determining the loyalty of individuals ...having access to restricted Atomic Energy data." Later, executive orders from both

President Eisenhower presents the National Security Medal to J. Edgar Hoover

Presidents Truman and Eisenhower gave the FBI responsibility for investigating allegations of disloyalty among federal employees. In these cases, the agency requesting the investigation made the final determination; the FBI only conducted the investigation and reported the results. Many suspected and convicted spies, such as Julius and Ethel Rosenberg, had been federal employees. Therefore, background investigations were considered to be just as vital as cracking major espionage cases.

Despite the threats to the United States of subversion and espionage, the FBI's extended jurisdiction, and the time-consuming nature of background investigations, the Bureau did not surpass the number of Agents it had during World War II--or its yearly wartime budget--until the Korean War in the early 1950s. After the Korean War ended, the number of Agents stabilized at about 6,200, while the budget began a steady climb in 1957.

Several factors converged to undermine domestic Communism in the 1950s. Situations like the Soviet defeat of the Hungarian rebellion in 1956 caused many members to abandon the American Communist Party. However, the FBI also played a role in diminishing Party influence. The Bureau was responsible for the investigation and arrest of alleged spies and Smith Act violators, most of whom were convicted. Through Hoover's speeches, articles, testimony, and books like Masters of Deceit, the FBI helped alert the public to the Communist threat.

The FBI's role in fighting crime also expanded in

An early Wanted poster

the postwar period through its assistance to state and local law enforcement and through increased jurisdictional responsibility. On March 14, 1950, the FBI began its "Ten Most Wanted Fugitives" List to increase law enforcement's ability to capture dangerous fugitives. Advances in forensic science and technical development enabled the FBI to devote a significant proportion of its resources to assisting state and local law enforcement agencies.

A dramatic example of aid to a state occurred after the midair explosion of a plane over Colorado in 1955. The FBI Laboratory examined hundreds of airplane parts, pieces of cargo, and the personal effects of passengers. It pieced together evidence of a bomb explosion from passenger luggage, then painstakingly looked into the backgrounds of the 44 victims. Ultimately, Agents identified the perpetrator and secured his confession, then turned the case over to Colorado authorities who successfully prosecuted it in a state court.

At the same time, Congress gave the FBI new federal laws with which to fight civil rights violations, racketeering, and gambling. These new laws included the Civil Rights Acts of 1960 and 1964; the 1961 Crimes Aboard Aircraft Act; an expanded Federal Fugitive Act; and the Sports Bribery Act of 1964.

Up to this time, the interpretation of federal civil rights statutes by the Supreme Court was so narrow that few crimes, however heinous, qualified to be investigated by federal agents.

The turning point in federal civil rights actions occurred in the summer of 1964, with the murder of voting registration workers Michael Schwerner, Andrew Goodman, and James Chaney near Philadelphia, Mississippi. At the Department of Justice's request, the FBI conducted the investigation as it had in previous, less-publicized racial incidents. The case against the perpetrators took years to go through the courts. Only after 1966, when the Supreme Court made it clear that federal law could be used to prosecute civil rights violations, were seven men found guilty. By the late 1960s, the confluence of unambiguous federal authority and local support for civil rights prosecutions allowed the FBI to play an influential role in enabling African Americans to vote, serve on juries, and use public accommodations on an equal basis.

Other civil rights investigations included the assassination of Martin Luther King, Jr., with the arrest of James Earl Ray, and the murder of Medger Evers, Mississippi Field Secretary of the NAACP, with the arrest of Byron De La Beckwith who, after two acquittals, was finally found guilty in 1994.

Involvement of the FBI in organized crime investigations also was hampered by the lack of possible federal laws covering crimes perpetrated by racketeers. After Prohibition, many mob activities were carried out locally, or if interstate, they did not constitute major violations within the Bureau's jurisdiction.

An impetus for federal legislation occurred in 1957 with the discovery by Sergeant Croswell of the New York State Police that many of the best known mobsters in the United States had met together in upstate New York. The FBI collected information on all the individuals identified at the meeting, confirming the existence of a national organized-crime network. However, it was not until an FBI Agent persuaded mob insider Joseph Valachi to testify that the public learned firsthand of the nature of La Cosa Nostra, the American "mafia."

On the heels of Valachi's disclosures, Congress passed two new laws to strengthen federal racketeering and gambling statutes that had been passed in the 1950s and early 1960s to aid the Bureau's fight against mob influence. The Omnibus Crime Control and Safe Streets Act of 1968 provided for the use of court-ordered electronic surveillance in the investigation of certain specified violations. The Racketeer Influenced and Corrupt Organizations (RICO) Statute of 1970 allowed organized groups to be prosecuted for all of their diverse criminal activities, without the crimes being linked by a perpetrator or all-encompassing conspiracy. Along with greater use of Agents for undercover work by the late 1970s, these provisions helped the FBI develop cases that, in the 1980s, put almost all the major traditional crime family heads in prison.

By the end of the 1960s, the Bureau employed 6,703 Special Agents and 9,320 Support Personnel in 58 field offices and twelve Legal Attache offices.

A national tragedy produced another expansion of FBI jurisdiction. When President Kennedy was assassinated, the crime was a local homicide; no federal law addressed the murder of a President. Nevertheless, President Lyndon B. Johnson tasked the Bureau with conducting the investigation. Congress then passed a new law to ensure that any such act in the future would be a federal crime. ★

THE VIETNAM WAR ERA
(1960s – 1970s)

President Kennedy's assassination introduced the violent aspect of the era known as the "Sixties." This period, which actually lasted into the mid-1970s, was characterized by idealism, but also by increased urban crime and a propensity for some groups to resort to violence in challenging the "establishment."

Most Americans objecting to involvement in Vietnam or to other policies wrote to Congress or carried peace signs in orderly demonstrations. Nevertheless, in 1970 alone, an estimated 3,000 bombings and 50,000 bomb threats occurred in the United States.

Opposition to the war in Vietnam brought together numerous anti-establishment groups and gave them a common goal. The convergence of crime, violence, civil rights issues, and potential national security issues ensured that the FBI played a significant role during this troubled period.

Presidents Johnson and Nixon and Director Hoover shared with many Americans a perception of the potential dangers to this country from some who opposed its policies in Vietnam.

The United States was confronted with "a new style in conspiracy — conspiracy that is extremely subtle and devious and hence difficult to understand...a conspiracy reflected by questionable moods and attitudes, by unrestrained individualism, by nonconformism in dress and speech, even by obscene language, rather than by formal membership in specific organizations."

As Hoover observed in a 1966 PTA Magazine article, the United States was confronted with "a new style in conspiracy--conspiracy that is extremely subtle and devious and hence difficult to understand...a conspiracy reflected by questionable moods and attitudes, by unrestrained individualism, by nonconformism in dress and speech, even by obscene language, rather than by formal membership in specific organizations."

The New Left movement's "romance with violence" involved, among others, four young men living in Madison, Wisconsin. Antiwar sentiment was widespread at the University of Wisconsin (UW), where two of them were students. During the very early morning of August 24, 1970, the four used a powerful homemade bomb to blow up Sterling Hall, which housed the Army Math Research Center at UW. A graduate student was killed and three others were injured.

That crime occurred a few months after National Guardsmen killed four students and wounded several others during an antiwar demonstration at Kent State University. The FBI investigated both incidents. Together, these events helped end the "romance with violence" for all but a handful of hard core New Left revolutionaries. Draft dodging and property damage had been tolerable to many antiwar sympathizers. Deaths were not.

By 1971, with few exceptions, the most extreme members of the antiwar movement concentrated on more peaceable tactics, such as the publication of The Pentagon Papers. However, the violent Weathermen and its successor groups continued to challenge the FBI into the 1980s.

No specific guidelines for FBI Agents covering national security investigations had been developed by the Administration or Congress; these, in fact, were not issued until 1976. Therefore, the FBI addressed the threats from the militant "New Left" as it had those from Communists in the 1950s and the KKK in the 1960s. It used both traditional investigative techniques and counterintelligence programs ("Cointelpro") to counteract domestic terrorism and conduct investigations of individuals and organizations who threatened terroristic violence. Wiretapping and other intrusive techniques were discouraged by Hoover in the mid-1960s and eventually

The FBI used traditional investigative techniques and counterintelligence programs to counteract domestic terrorism and conduct investigations of individuals and organizations who threatened terroristic violence.

J. Edgar Hoover

Director, Gray appointed the first women as Special Agents since the 1920s.

Shortly after Gray became Acting Director, five men were arrested photographing documents at the Democratic National Headquarters in the Watergate Office Building in Washington, D.C. The break-in had been authorized by Republican Party officials. Within hours, the White House began its effort to cover up its role, and the new Acting FBI Director was inadvertently drawn into it. FBI Agents undertook a thorough investigation of the break-in and related events. However, when Gray's questionable personal role was revealed, he withdrew his name from the Senate's consideration to be Director. He was replaced hours after he resigned on April 27, 1973, by William Ruckleshaus, a former Congressman and the first head of the Environmental Protection Agency, who remained until Clarence Kelley's appointment as Director on July 9, 1973. Kelley, who was Kansas City Police Chief when he received the appointment, had been an FBI Agent from 1940 to 1961. ★

Clarence Kelley

were forbidden completely unless they conformed to the Omnibus Crime Control Act. Hoover formally terminated all "Cointelpro" operations on April 28, 1971.

FBI Director J. Edgar Hoover died on May 2, 1972, just shy of 48 years as the FBI Director. He was 77. The next day his body lay in state in the Rotunda of the Capitol, an honor accorded only 21 other Americans.

Hoover's successor would have to contend with the complex turmoil of that troubled time. In 1972, unlike 1924 when Attorney General Harlan Fiske Stone selected Hoover, the President appointed the FBI Director with confirmation by the Senate. President Nixon appointed L. Patrick Gray as Acting Director the day after Hoover's death. After retiring from a distinguished Naval career, Gray had continued in public service as the Department of Justice's Assistant Attorney General for the Civil Division. As Acting

AFTERMATH OF WATERGATE
(1970s)

Three days after Director Kelley's appointment, top aides in the Nixon Administration resigned amid charges of White House efforts to obstruct justice in the Watergate case. Vice President Spiro T. Agnew resigned in October, following charges of tax evasion. Then, following impeachment hearings that were broadcast over television to the American public throughout 1974, President Nixon resigned on August 9, 1974. Vice President Gerald R. Ford was sworn in as President that same day. In granting an unconditional pardon to ex-President Nixon one month later, he vowed to heal the nation.

The FBI's modern day headquarters

Patty Hearst's wanted poster

Director Kelley similarly sought to restore public trust in the FBI and in law enforcement. He instituted numerous policy changes that targeted the training and selection of FBI and law enforcement leaders, the procedures of investigative intelligence collection, and the prioritizing of criminal programs. All of this was done while continuing open investigations. One such case was the Patty Hearst kidnapping investigation.

In 1974, Kelley instituted Career Review Boards and programs to identify and train potential managers. For upper management of the entire law enforcement community, the FBI, in cooperation with the International Association of Chiefs of Police and the Major Cities Chief Administrators, started the National Executive Institute, which provided high-level executive training and encouraged future operational cooperation.

Kelley also responded to scrutiny by Congress and the media on whether FBI methods of collecting intelligence in domestic security and counterintelligence investigations abridged Constitutional rights.

The FBI had traditionally used its own criteria for intelligence collection, based on executive orders and blanket authority granted by attorney generals.

After congressional hearings, Attorney General Edward Levi established finely detailed guidelines for the first time. The guidelines for FBI foreign counterintelligence investigations went into effect on March 10, 1976, and for domestic security investigations on April 5, 1976 (The latter were superseded March 21, 1983).

Kelley's most significant management innovation, however, was implementing the concept of "Quality over Quantity" investigations. He directed each field office to set priorities based on the types of cases most important in its territory and to concentrate resources on those priority matters. Strengthening the "Quality over Quantity" concept, the FBI as a whole established three national priorities: foreign counterintelligence, organized crime, and white-collar crime. To handle the last priority, the Bureau intensified its recruitment of accountants. It also stepped up its use of undercover operations in major cases.

During Kelley's tenure as Director, the FBI made a strong effort to develop an Agent force with more women and one that was more reflective of the ethnic composition of the United States. By the late 1970s nearly 8,000 Special Agents and 11,000 Support Employees worked in 59 Field Offices and 13 Legal Attache offices. ★

An FBI field agent

RISE OF INTERNATIONAL CRIME (1980s)

William H. Webster

In 1978, Director Kelley resigned and was replaced by former federal Judge William H. Webster. At the time of his appointment, Webster was serving as Judge of the U.S. Court of Appeals for the Eighth Circuit. He had previously been a Judge of the U.S. District Court for the Eastern District of Missouri. Also in 1978, the FBI began using laser technology in the Identification Division to detect latent crime scene fingerprints.

In 1982, following an explosion of terrorist incidents worldwide, Webster made counterterrorism a fourth national priority. He also expanded FBI efforts in the three others: foreign counterintelligence, organized crime, and white-collar crime. Part of this expansion was the creation of the National Center for the Analysis of Violent Crime.

The FBI solved so many espionage cases during the mid-1980s that the press dubbed 1985 "the year of the spy." The most serious espionage damage uncovered by the FBI was perpetrated by the John Walker spy ring and by former National Security Agency employee William Pelton.

Throughout the 1980s, the illegal drug trade severely challenged the resources of American law enforcement. To ease this challenge, in 1982 the Attorney General gave the FBI concurrent jurisdiction with the Drug Enforcement Administration (DEA) over narcotics violations in the United States. The expanded Department of Justice attention to drug crimes resulted in the confiscation of millions of dollars in controlled substances, the arrests of major narcotics figures, and the dismantling of important drug rings. One of the most publicized, dubbed "the Pizza Connection" case, involved the heroin trade in the United States and Italy. It resulted in 18 convictions, including a former leader of the Sicilian Mafia. Then Assistant U.S. Attorney Louis J. Freeh, who was to be appointed FBI Director in 1993, was key to prosecutive successes in the case.

John Walker

Public corruption was attacked nationwide. Convictions resulting from FBI investigations included members of Congress, the judiciary, and state legislatures in California and South Carolina.

In 1989, the Department of Justice authorized the FBI to arrest terrorists, drug traffickers, and other fugitives abroad without the consent of the foreign country in which they resided.

The FBI's Hostage Rescue Team

On another front, Webster strengthened the FBI's response to white-collar crimes. Public corruption was attacked nationwide. Convictions resulting from FBI investigations included members of Congress (ABSCAM), the judiciary (GREYLORD), and state legislatures in California and South Carolina. A major investigation culminating in 1988 unveiled corruption in defense procurement (ILLWIND).

As the United States faced a financial crisis in the failures of savings and loan associations during the 1980s, the FBI uncovered instances of fraud that lay behind many of those failures. It was perhaps the single largest investigative effort undertaken by the FBI to that date: from investigating 10 bank failures in 1981, it had 282 bank failures under investigation by February 1987. Resources to investigate fraud during the savings and loan crisis were provided by the Financial Institution Reform, Recovery and Enhancement Act.

In 1984, the FBI acted as lead agency for security of the Los Angeles Olympics. In the course of its efforts to anticipate and prepare for acts of terrorism and street crime, it built important bridges of interaction and cooperation with local, state, and other federal agencies, as well as agencies of other countries. It also unveiled the FBI's Hostage Rescue Team as a domestic force capable of responding to complex hostage situations such as tragically occurred in Munich at the 1972 games.

Perhaps as a result of the Bureau's emphasis on combatting terrorism, such acts within the United States decreased dramatically during the 1980s. In 1986, Congress had expanded FBI jurisdiction to cover terrorist acts against U.S. citizens outside the U.S. boundaries. Later, in 1989, the Department of Justice authorized the FBI to arrest terrorists, drug traffickers, and other fugitives abroad without the

consent of the foreign country in which they resided.

Expanded resources were not limited to "established" crime areas like terrorism and violent crime. In 1984, the FBI established the Computer Analysis and Response Team (CART) to retrieve evidence from computers. CART would become fully operational in 1991.

On May 26, 1987, Judge Webster left the FBI to become Director of the Central Intelligence Agency. Executive Assistant Director John E. Otto became Acting Director and served in that position until November 2, 1987. During his tenure, Acting Director Otto designated drug investigations as the FBI's fifth national priority.

On November 2, 1987, former federal Judge William Steele Sessions was sworn in as FBI Director. Prior to his appointment as FBI Director, Sessions served as the Chief Judge of the U.S. District Court for the Western District of Texas. He had previously served as a District Judge and as U.S. Attorney for that district.

CART was established to retrieve evidence from computers

Under Director Sessions, crime prevention efforts, in place since Director Kelley's tenure, were expanded to include a drug demand reduction program. FBI offices nationwide began working closely with local school and civic groups to educate young people to the dangers of drugs. Subsequent nationwide community outreach efforts under that program evolved and expanded through such initiatives as the Adopt-A-School/Junior G-Man Program. The expansion in initiatives required a larger workforce and by 1988, the FBI employed 9,663 Special Agents and 13,651 Support Employees in 58 Field Offices and 15 Legal Attaches. ★

THE END OF THE COLD WAR (1989 – 1993)

The dismantling of the Berlin Wall in November 1989 electrified the world and dramatically rang up the Iron Curtain on the final act in the Cold War: the formal dissolution of the Soviet Union, which occurred on December 25, 1991.

While world leaders scrambled to reposition their foreign policies and redefine national security parameters, the FBI responded as an agency in January 1992 by reassigning 300 Special Agents from foreign counterintelligence duties to violent crime investigations across the country. It was an unprecedented opportunity to intensify efforts in burgeoning domestic crime problems--and at the same time to rethink and retool FBI national security programs in counterintelligence and counterterrorism.

In response to a 40-percent increase in crimes of violence over the previous 10 years, Director Sessions had designated the investigation of violent crime as the FBI's sixth national priority program in 1989. By November 1991 the FBI had created "Operation Safe Streets" in Washington, D.C.--a concept of federal, state, and local police task forces targeting fugitives and gangs. Therefore, it was now ready to expand this operational assistance to police nationwide.

National security was no longer defined as the containment of communism and the prevention of nuclear war.

At the same time, the FBI Laboratory helped change the face of violent criminal identification. Its breakthrough use of DNA technology enabled genetic crime-scene evidence to positively identify--or rule out--suspects by comparing their particular DNA patterns. This unique identifier enabled the creation of a national DNA Index, similar to the fingerprint index, which had been implemented in 1924.

The FBI also strengthened its response to white-collar crimes. Popularized as "crime in the suites," these nonviolent crimes had steadily increased as automation in and deregulation of industries had created new environments for fraud. Resources were, accordingly, redirected to combat the new wave of large-scale insider bank fraud and financial crimes; to address criminal sanctions in new federal environmental legislation; and to establish long-term investigations of complex health care frauds.

At the same time, the FBI reassessed its strategies in defending national security, now no longer defined as the containment of communism and the prevention of nuclear war.

By creating the National Security Threat List, which was approved by the Attorney General in 1991, it changed its approach from defending against hostile intelligence agencies to protecting U.S. information and technologies. It thus identified all countries--not just hostile intelligence services--that pose a continuing and serious intelligence threat to the United States. It also defined expanded threat issues, including the proliferation of chemical, biological, and nuclear weapons; the loss of critical technologies; and the improper collection of trade secrets and proprietary information. As President Clinton was to note in 1994, with the dramatic expansion of the global economy "national security now means economic security."

Two events occurred in late 1992 and early 1993 that were to have a major impact on FBI policies and operations. In August 1992, the FBI responded to the shooting death of Deputy U.S. Marshal William Degan, who was killed at Ruby Ridge, Idaho, while participating in a surveillance of federal fugitive Randall Weaver. In the course of the standoff, Weaver's wife was accidentally shot and killed by an FBI sniper.

Eight months later, at a remote compound outside Waco, Texas, FBI Agents sought to end a 51-day standoff with members of a heavily armed religious sect who had killed four officers of the Bureau of Alcohol, Tobacco and Firearms. Instead, as Agents watched in horror, the compound burned to the ground from fires lit by members of the sect. Eighty persons, including children, died in the blaze.

These two events set the stage for public and congressional inquiries into the FBI's ability to respond to crisis situations.

On July 19, 1993, following allegations of ethics violations committed by Director Sessions, President Clinton removed him from office and appointed Deputy Director Floyd I. Clarke as Acting FBI Director. The President noted that Director Sessions' most significant achievement was broadening the FBI to include more women and minorities. ★

PREPARING FOR THE FUTURE
(1993 – Present)

Louis J. Freeh was sworn in as Director of the FBI on September 1, 1993. He had served as an FBI Agent from 1975 to 1981 in the New York City Field Office and at FBI Headquarters before leaving to join the U.S. Attorney's Office for the Southern District of New York. Here Freeh rose quickly and prosecuted many major FBI cases, includ-

Louis J. Freeh

ing the notorious "Pizza Connection" case and the "VANPAC" mail bomb case. He was appointed a U.S. District Court Judge for the Southern District of New York in 1991. On July 20, 1993, President Clinton nominated him to be FBI Director. He was confirmed by the U.S. Senate on August 6, 1993.

Freeh began his tenure with a clearly articulated agenda that would respond both to deepening crime problems and to a climate of government downsizing. In his oath of office speech he called for new levels of cooperation among law enforcement agencies, both at home and abroad, and he announced his intention to restructure the FBI in order to maximize its operational response to crime.

A major reorganization to streamline Headquarters operations of the FBI was announced. Selected divisions and offices were merged, reorganized, or abolished, cutting many management positions. Soon after, Freeh ordered the transfer of 600 Special Agents serving in administrative positions to investigative positions in field offices. To revitalize an aging Agent work force, Freeh gained approval to end a 2-year hiring freeze on new Agents. In continuation of the FBI's commitment to the advancement of minorities and women within the ranks of the organization, in October 1993, Freeh appointed the first woman, the first man of Hispanic descent, and the second man of African-American descent to be named Assistant Director. These, and other changes, strengthened the FBI's traditionally high requirements for personal conduct and ethics, and established a "bright line"

between what would be acceptable and what would not.

Director Freeh emphasized law enforcement cooperation as a necessary way to combat domestic and international crime. For example, Freeh was given a simultaneous appointment to serve as Director of the Department of Justice's new Office of Investigative Agency Policies. From this position, he has been able to work effectively with law enforcement agencies within the Department of Justice to develop close cooperation on criminal law enforcement issues, including sharing information on drug intelligence, automation, firearms, and aviation support. Internationally, the FBI had to meet the globalization of crime. For example, on June 7, 1999, the FBI placed Usama Bin Laden on the "Ten Most Wanted" List for his alleged involvement in the 1998 bombings of United States embassies in Africa.

The globalization of crime required international cooperation. In the summer of 1994, Freeh led a delegation of high-level diplomatic and federal law enforcement officials to meet with senior officials of 11 European nations on international crime issues. Earlier, he traveled to Sicily to honor his late friend and colleague Giovanni Falcone, who had been killed in a bomb blast with his wife and three bodyguards the year before. On the steps of the Palatine Chapel of the Palace of the Normans, in the face of the Mafia presence, Freeh challenged the Sicilian people "to oppose them with your minds and hearts and the rule of law." This message was to be repeated and strengthened the following year in the new democratic capitals of Russia and Eastern Europe.

At the outset, Richard Holbrooke, U.S. Ambassador to Germany, declared, "This is the evolving American foreign policy. Law Enforcement is at the forefront of our national interest in this part of the world." Meetings were held with officials of Russia, Germany, the Czech Republic, the Slovak Republic, Hungary, Poland, the Ukraine, Austria, Lithuania, Latvia, and Estonia. On July 4, 1994, Director Freeh officially announced the historic opening of an FBI Legal Attache Office in Moscow, the old seat of Russian communism. By the latter half of 2000, the FBI had Legats in other former-Soviet cities including Budapest, Hungary; Kiev, Ukraine; Warsaw, Poland; and Bucharest, Romania.

The International Law Enforcement Academy

Subsequently, international leaders and law enforcement officials have focused on ways to strengthen security measures against possible theft of nuclear weapons and nuclear materials from Russia and other former republics of the Soviet Union. They have sharpened joint efforts against organized crime, drug trafficking, and terrorism. They have also strongly supported the FBI's efforts to institute standardized training of international police in investigative processes, ethics, leadership, and professionalism: in April 1995, the International Law Enforcement Academy opened its doors in Budapest, Hungary. Staffed by FBI and other law enforcement trainers, the academy offers five eight-week courses a year, based on the FBI's National Academy concept.

The FBI spearheaded initiatives to prepare for both domestic and foreign lawlessness in the 21st century. For example, the law enforcement made an effort to ensure its ability, in the face of telecommunications advances, to carry out court-authorized electronic surveillance in major investigations affecting public safety and national security. This ability was secured when Congress passed the Communications Assistance for Law Enforcement Act in October 1994. In 1998, to combat cybercrime, the National Infrastructure Protection Center (NIPC) was established. Located in FBI Headquarters, NIPC brings together representatives from U.S. government agencies, state and local government, and private enterprises to protect the nation's critical infrastructures.

Investigative efforts through the years 1993 to 1996 paid off in successful investigations as diverse as the World Trade Center bombing in New York City (Ramzi Yousef); the Oklahoma City bombing; the Archer Daniels Midland international price-fixing conspiracies;

Ramzi Yousef

the attempted theft of Schering-Plough and Merck pharmaceutical trade secrets; and the arrests of Mexican drug trafficker Juan Garcia-Abrego and Russian crime boss Vyacheslav Ivankov.

Congress further expanded the FBI's ability to investigate acts such as espionage, through the Economic Espionage Act of 1996, abortion clinic violence, through the Freedom of Access to Clinic Entrances Act of 1994, and interstate stalking and spousal abuse, through part of the Violent Crime Control and Law Enforcement Act of 1994. In 1996, the Health Insurance Portability and Accountability Act and the Economic Espionage Act were passed in the closing days of the 104th Session of Congress, then signed into law. These new statutes enabled the FBI to significantly strengthen its criminal programs in health care fraud and the theft of trade secrets and intellectual property.

Director Freeh initiated many changes to prepare for evolving criminal challenges, especially those challenges described in his FBI's Strategic Plan for 1998-2003. For example, he began construction of a new state-of-the-art FBI forensic laboratory. He formed the Critical Incident Response Group to deal efficiently with crisis situations. He also initiated a comprehensive and integrated FBI response to nuclear, biological, and chemical (NBC) crisis incidents when the FBI was designated lead law enforcement agency in NBC investigations. In June 2001, FBI Director Freeh retired from federal government service.

On September 4, 2001, Robert S. Mueller III became the Director of the FBI. On September 11, 2001, terror-

Robert S. Mueller

ists attacked the World Trade Center in New York City and the Pentagon in Washington D.C. In October, the FBI confronted another challenge: anthrax-laden letters. The FBI quickly committed all resources at its disposal to investigate the terrorist attacks, the anthrax-laden letters, and to prevent future incidents. To meet these and future challenges, Director Mueller announced a reorganization of FBI Headquarters.

The FBI's work on behalf of the American people is being carried out by some of the most dedicated and talented employees found anywhere in the world today. All are committed to combatting criminal activity through the Bureau's investigations, programs, and law enforcement services. They continue the mission of that first small group of Special Agents in 1908 who established a tradition of service that has become the Bureau's motto: Fidelity, Bravery, and Integrity. ★

The FBI's

TEN
MOST
WANTED

Fugitives

★　　　★　　　★　　　★　　　★

Although most people think that the Ten Most Wanted List has been around since the days of John Dillinger and Bonnie and Clyde, they're wrong. FBI Director J. Edgar Hoover actually started the list in 1950 in response to an inquiry by a United Press reporter who wanted to know who were the toughest guys the FBI wanted to capture.

The country's news media played a key role in the program, as they were the most efficient means of publicizing the names and descriptions of the fugitives on the list. Nine of the first twenty individuals on the list were apprehended due to the cooperation of our citizens. To this date, 144 of the top ten arrests have been credited to the public at large.

Representatives of the fifty six field offices of the FBI's Criminal Investigation Division choose the fugitives selected to be included on the list. In order to be selected, the fugitive must be considered to be a menace to society, and extremely dangerous. In addition, the FBI must feel that the publicity of inclusion on the list will be helpful in apprehending the fugitive.

A Top Tenner can be removed from the list if he or she is captured, surrenders or dies, if the charges against him are dropped, or if the fugitive no longer fits the Ten Most Wanted criteria. From time to time, the list has exceeded ten fugitives, due to special circumstances. This has happened eleven times to date. At the time this book was being printed, only eight people were on the list as two fugitives were apprehended in the last few days, and new criminals were not yet added.

Since its inception over fifty years ago, 472 people have made it to the Top Ten and 442 have been captured or located.

FBI TEN MOST WANTED
TERRORISM, MURDER

USAMA BIN LADEN
$25,000,000 REWARD

Murder of U.S. nationals outside the United States; Conspiracy to murder U.S. nationals outside the United States; Attack on a federal facility resulting in death

Date of photograph unknown

ALIASES: Usama Bin Muhammad Bin Ladin, Shaykh Usama Bin Ladin, the Prince, the Emir, Abu Abdallah, Mujahid Shaykh, Hajj, the Director

DESCRIPTION

DATE OF BIRTH: 1957	**HAIR:** Brown
PLACE OF BIRTH: Saudi Arabia	**EYES:** Brown
HEIGHT: 6'4" to 6'6"	**COMPLEXION:** Olive
BUILD: Thin	**SEX:** Male
OCCUPATIONS: Unknown	**NATIONALITY:** Saudi Arabian
SCARS AND MARKS: None	

REMARKS: Leader of a terrorist organization known as Al-Qaeda "The Base." He is left-handed and walks with a cane.

CAUTION
Usama Bin Laden is wanted in connection with the September 11, 2001 terrorist attacks and the August 7, 1998, bombings of the United States embassies in Dar Es Salaam, Tanzania and Nairobi,Kenya. These attacks killed thousands of people. In addition, Bin Laden is a suspect in other terrorist attacks throughout the world.
CONSIDERED ARMED AND DANGEROUS

INTERNATIONAL CRIME ALERT
USAMA BIN LADEN

Usama bin Laden is a 45 year-old "businessman" and son of one of Saudi Arabia's wealthiest families, and the coordinator of an international terrorist network believed to be responsible for numerous deadly attacks against American and Western targets.

Bin Laden formed the terrorist Al-Qaeda ("the base") organization in 1988, and it is believed to have operatives in as many as twenty countries. In 1998 bin Laden announced the establishment of "The International Islamic Front for Holy War Against Jews and Crusaders," an umbrella organization linking Islamic extremists in scores of countries around the world, including Egypt, Bangladesh and Pakistan. The group issued a religious edict upon its establishment: "The ruling to kill the Americans and their allies, civilians, and the military, is an individual duty for every Muslim who can do it in any country in which it is possible to do it, in order to liberate al-Aqsa Mosque and the Holy Mosque from their grip and in order for their armies to move out of all the lands of Islam, defeated, and unable to threaten any Muslim. This is in accordance with the words of Almighty G-d, and 'fight the pagans all together as they fight you all together,' and 'fight them until there is no more tumult or oppression, and there prevail justice and faith in G-d."

His militancy is traced back to the 1979 Soviet invasion of Afghanistan. Bin Laden's avowed goal from that time is to remove Western "infidels" from Muslim countries – the Russians from Afghanistan, the American military from Saudi Arabia and other points in the Gulf – the downfall of many governments of Muslim states, and for the destruction of the United States and its allies.

Bin Laden is the son of the Yemeni-born owner of a leading Saudi construction company. Born into great wealth, he is believed to have inherited as much as $300 million when his father died in the 1960's. From 1979, bin Laden began raising money for the Mujahadeen forces fighting the Soviets in Afghanistan, and gradually became more and more affiliated with Egyptian Islamic extremist groups, such as Egyptian Islamic Jihad. From the mid-1980's bin Laden began to establish training camps in Afghanistan, initially for the war in Afghanistan, but later to fight against other targets worldwide. He has attracted thousands of recruits from Saudi Arabia, Algeria, Egypt, Yemen, Pakistan and Sudan.

Reportedly, bin Laden's anti-Americanism intensified during the Gulf War, when U.S. troops were stationed in Saudi Arabia. According to The New York Times: "The presence of American soldiers in Saudi Arabia, the birthplace of the Prophet Muhammad and the home of the two holiest Muslim shrines, enraged Mr. bin Laden and other Arab militants." He and his associates also blamed the U.S. support for Israel as anti-Islam.

In 1994 Saudi Arabia stripped bin Laden's citizenship, citing his opposition to the Saudi King and leadership and expelled him from the country. He then went to Khartoum, Sudan (where he owns numerous businesses), but under U.S. pressure was expelled in 1996 and relocated to Afghanistan. Bin Laden is on the FBI's list of 10 most-wanted criminals, and the State Department offered a $5 million reward for his arrest following the August 1998 embassy bombings. The United Nations imposed economic sanctions on the Taliban regime in Afghanistan in 1999 for harboring bin Laden, and many nations, including the U.S. have frozen assets owned by bin Laden and his senior associates. The reward has been increased to $25 million after the September 11, 2001 events.

Bin Laden has been thought to finance, inspire or directly organize various terrorist attacks. In one way or another his name has been linked to the killings of Western tourists by militant Islamic groups in Egypt, bombings in France by Islamic extremist Algerians, the maintenance of a safe-house in Pakistan for Ramzi Ahmed Yousef, the convicted mastermind of the 1993 World Trade Center bombing, and sheltering Sheikh Omar Abd Al-Rahman (the Blind Sheikh), who was also convicted in the World Trade Center bombing. He has also been linked to the 1992 bombings of a hotel in Yemen, which killed two Australians, but was supposedly targeted against American soldiers stationed there; the 1995 detonation of a car bomb in Riyadh, Saudi Arabia; the 1995 truck bomb in Dhahran, Saudi Arabia that killed 19 U.S. servicemen; and the 1995 assassination attempt on Egyptian President Hosni Mubarak. Bin Laden has been directly connected to the August 7, 1998 bombing of the U.S. embassies in Nairobi, Kenya and Dar-es-Salaam, Tanzania, killing 224 people, and the October 2000 attack of the U.S. destroyer ship Cole in Yemen.

Most recently, he has been accused of masterminding the September 11, 2001 attack on the Pentagon and World Trade Center in New York City.

Bin Laden has made no secret of his anti-American, anti-Western and anti-Israel sentiments. In fact, he has been outspoken on these topics, issuing theological rulings calling for Muslims to attack Americans and threatening terrorism against related targets.

FBI TEN MOST WANTED
MURDER

GLEN STEWART GODWIN
$50,000 REWARD

Unlawful flight to avoid confinement – murder, escape

WANTED BY THE FBI

Photograph taken in 1991

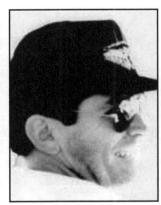
Photograph taken in 1991

Age enhanced photograph

ALIASES: Michael Carrera, Miguel Carrera, Michael Carmen, Glen Godwin, Glen S. Godwin, Dennis H. McWilliams, Dennis Harold McWilliams

DESCRIPTION

DATE OF BIRTH: June 26, 1958	**SCARS, MARKS, TATTOOS:** None known.
PLACE OF BIRTH: Miami, Florida	**HAIR:** Black/Salt and Pepper
HEIGHT: 6'0"	**EYES:** Green
WEIGHT: 200 lbs	**SEX:** Male
BUILD : Medium	**RACE:** White
OCCUPATIONS: Self-employed in tool supplies, mechanic, construction worker	**NATIONALITY:** American

REMARKS: Godwin is fluent in Spanish and may be traveling throughout Central and South America. He is thought to be involved in narcotics distribution.

CAUTION

Glen Stewart Godwin is being sought for his 1987 escape from Folsom State Prison in California, where he was serving a lengthy sentence for murder. Later in 1987, Godwin was arrested for drug trafficking in Puerta Vallarta, Mexico. After being convicted, he was sent to a prison in Guadalajara. In April of 1991, Godwin allegedly murdered a fellow inmate and then escaped five months later.

SHOULD BE CONSIDERED ARMED AND DANGEROUS

FBI TEN MOST WANTED
FOR MURDER

DONALD EUGENE WEBB
$50,000 REWARD

Unlawful flight to avoid prosecution – murder; attempted burglary

WANTED BY THE FBI

Photograph taken in 1979

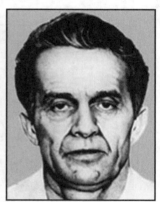

Age enhanced photograph

ALIAS: Sid Shajbra

DESCRIPTION

DATE OF BIRTH: July 14, 1931
PLACE OF BIRTH: Oklahoma City, Oklahoma
HEIGHT: 5'9"
WEIGHT: 165 lbs
BUILD: Medium
OCCUPATION(S): Butcher, car salesman, jewelry salesman, restaurant manager, vending machine repairman
COMPLEXION: Medium

SCARS, MARKS, TATTOOS: May have a small scar on his right cheek and his right forearm. He may have the following tattoos: "DON" on the web of his right hand and "ANN" on his chest.
HAIR: Gray-brown
EYES: Brown
SEX: Male
RACE: White
NATIONALITY: American

REMARKS: Donald Eugene Webb, who is considered a career criminal and master of assumed identities, specializes in the burglary of jewelry stores. He is reportedly allergic to penicillin, a lover of dogs, a flashy dresser and a big tipper.

CAUTION

Donald Eugene Webb is being sought in connection with the murder of a police chief in Pennsylvania who was shot twice at close range after being brutally beaten about the head and face with a blunt instrument.

SHOULD BE CONSIDERED ARMED AND DANGEROUS

FBI TEN MOST WANTED
DRUG SMUGGLING

JAMES SPENCER SPRINGETTE
$50,000 REWARD

Conspiracy to import cocaine hydrochloride and cocaine base; conspiracy to distribute cocaine; conspiracy to launder monetary instruments

WANTED BY THE FBI, U.S. CUSTOMS, U.S. MARSHALS

ALIASES: Elmo Brady, Elmo Brandy, Kyle Pierce, Elmo Spencer, Kent Worwell, Kent Worrel, Kent Worral, Shawn Pickering, Brian Miller, Jimmy Springette, Jimi Springette, James Spencer, Efram Zoran Johnson, Everson Weberson, Spencer Springette, "Jimmy", "Juice", "Seagal", "Jimmy the Juice", "Uncle"

DESCRIPTION

DATES OF BIRTH USED: August 18, 1960; August 16, 1960	**EYES:** Brown
	SCARS, MARKS, TATTOOS: None known
PLACE OF BIRTH: St. Thomas, U.S. Virgin Islands	**SEX:** Male
HEIGHT: 5'11"	**RACE:** Black
WEIGHT: 240 lbs	**NATIONALITY:** American
OCCUPATION: Unknown	**NCIC:** W401996856
HAIR: Black	

CAUTION

James Spencer Springette is wanted for his alleged involvement in a large drug-smuggling organization known as the "Island Boys". Springette has allegedly been the head of this group since at least 1991. He is thought to be responsible for the importation of large amounts of cocaine from Colombia which is reportedly air dropped into the Caribbean, divided into smaller quantities, and transported by couriers to Atlanta, Georgia, and other cities in the United States. Springette was indicted in the Southern District of Georgia in October of 1998 for conspiracy to import and distribute cocaine, and money laundering. On January 30, 1999, Springette was arrested in Medellin, Colombia, on a provisional arrest warrant secured in the Southern District of Georgia. In March of 2000, while in prison awaiting extradition to the United States, Springette escaped from La Picota maximum security prison in Bogota, Colombia, and remains a fugitive. He was added to the FBI's Ten Most Wanted list in April, 2002.

CONSIDERED ARMED AND DANGEROUS

INTERNATIONAL CRIME ALERT
JAMES SPENCER SPRINGETTE

On October 8, 1998, a warrant of arrest was issued for James Spencer SPRINGETTE for conspiracy to violate Title 21 United States Code, Section 963 (Importation of Cocaine into the United States). SPRINGETTE is the leader of the "Island Boys" drug smuggling organization. SPRINGETTE is linked to a seizure of over 10,000 kilograms of cocaine, acts of violence including two murders, shooting a police officer in the British Virgin Islands, and the beating of another police officer, after armed men hijacked a prison bus and freed two Colombian nationals associated with the Island Boys. In January 1999, SPRINGETTE was arrested in Colombia pursuant to a provisional arrest warrant. While pending extradition, SPRINGETTE escaped custody from a prison in Bogota, Colombia and he remains a fugitive. SPRINGETTE is believed to and should be considered armed and dangerous.

James Spencer Springette is a U.S. citizen born on August 16th, or August 18th, 1960, in the U.S. Virgin Islands. He is a black male, five feet eleven inches tall, and weighs 240 pounds. He has black hair and black eyes. He has a U.S. Virgin Islands driver's license and a passport from the Federation of St. Kitts and Nevis in the name of Elmo Brandy. Besides Elmo Brandy, he has used the names Elmo Spencer, Kyle Pierce, Kent Worwell, and Shawn Pickering. He is also known as "Jimmy the Juice." He should be considered armed and dangerous.

CASE DETAILS: Cocaine. Each year it takes the lives of thousands of people and destroys the health of thousands more. A major smuggler of this illegal drug is James Spencer Springette. U.S. authorities have linked him directly to the smuggling of more than forty-thousand kilograms of cocaine into the U.S. from Colombia in recent years. Springette maintains a large, Colombian-based cocaine distribution network through the use of fraud and violence, including murder. He is wanted for his part in a 1996 shootout in the British Virgin Islands that left a police officer blind in one eye. He is suspected in the escape of two Colombian drug-traffickers from jail in the British Virgin Islands in 1998. In October 1998, Springette was indicted by a federal court in Georgia for conspiracy to import cocaine, money laundering, and other offenses. He is believed to be operating in the U.S. Virgin Islands, British Virgin Islands, Venezuela, and Colombia. American authorities are seeking his extradition.

A substantial reward is available for those providing information leading to Springette's arrest.

If you have any information concerning James Spencer Springette, you should contact the nearest U.S. embassy or consulate, or call the U.S. Marshals Service at 1-800-336-0102, or contact the nearest U.S. Customs office or call the U.S. Customs National Law Enforcement Center at 1-800-BE ALERT. The identity of all informants will be kept confidential.

FBI TEN MOST WANTED
MURDER, DRUG DISTRIBUTION

JAMES J. BULGER
$1,000,000 REWARD

Racketeering Influenced and Corrupt Organizations (RICO) – Murder (19 counts), Conspiracy to commit murder, Conspiracy to commit extortion, narcotics distribution, Conspiracy to commit money laundering; Extortion; Money laundering

Photograph taken in 1994

ALIASES: Thomas F. Baxter, Mark Shapeton, Jimmy Bulger, James Joseph Bulger, James J. Bulger, Jr., James Joseph Bulger, Jr., Tom Harris, Tam Marshall, "Whitey"

DESCRIPTION

DATE OF BIRTH: September 3, 1929
PLACE OF BIRTH: Boston, Massachusetts
HEIGHT: 5'7" to 5'9"
WEIGHT: 150 to 160 pounds
BUILD: Medium
OCCUPATIONS: Unknown

SCARS AND MARKS: None known
HAIR: White/Silver
EYES: Blue
COMPLEXION: Light
SEX: Male
NATIONALITY: American

REMARKS: Bulger is an avid reader with an interest in history. He is known to frequent libraries and historic sites. Bulger is currently on the heart medication Atenolol (50 mg) and maintains his physical fitness by walking on beaches and in parks with his female companion, Catherine Elizabeth Greig. Bulger and Greig love animals and may frequent animal shelters. Bulger has been known to alter his appearance through the use of disguises. He has traveled extensively throughout the United States, Europe, Canada, and Mexico.

CAUTION

James J. Bulger is being sought for his role in numerous murders committed from the early 1970s through the mid-1980s in connection with his leadership of an organized crime group that allegedly controlled extortion, drug deals, and other illegal activities in the Boston, Massachusetts, area. He has a violent temper and is known to carry a knife at all times.
CONSIDERED ARMED AND DANGEROUS

INTERNATIONAL CRIME ALERT
JAMES "WHITEY" BULGER

Photograph altered in 2000

Not only is Whitey Bulger an FBI Top Tenner, but is also the brother of the former president of the Massachusetts State Senate. His real claim to fame however is the fact that has been indicted for nineteen murders that took place throughout the Boston area over a period of many years.

Bulger, who for many years was an informer for the FBI, has been a fugitive for more than six years. He is reputed to be the former leader of the Winter Hill Gang, which perpetrated numerous heinous crimes over an extended period of time. Bulger started his criminal career early in life, and was first convicted of bank robbery and sentenced to imprisonment in Alcatraz. He obtained an early release by volunteering to be a guinea pig for LSD experiments.

James Bulger, got his nickname Whitey as a towheaded blond boy growing up in South Boston, a predominantly Irish-American tough neighborhood. James and his brother Billy who is currently the President of The University of Massachusetts, went to Catholic school in Southie as their neighborhood was known. While brother Billy was graduating from Boston College with honors and then on to law school, Jimmy was robbing banks in Massachusetts,

Indiana and Rhode Island. He spent a total of nine years in Federal prisons where he became an even more hardened criminal.

Upon his release from prison at the age of 35, his brother Billy got him a job as a janitor in a courthouse. He didn't stay at this menial job very long, but shortly became the leader of a notorious gang of criminals known as the Winter Hill Gang. Over the next 40 years, Jimmy Bulger built a crime organization rivaling any in the country for discipline and profitability. He and his organization made millions in the 1980s when the bulk of the drug trafficking activity switched from New York to Boston.

During the Big Dig, the excavation of a large section of downtown Boston, six bodies were unearthed that are believed to be victims of the Winter Hill Gang. Whitey Bulger has been indicted for his involvement in these and 13 other murders. He is believed to be traveling with a female companion Catherine Greig. They have been seen in Wyoming, Arizona and California, but it is thought that they are currently hiding out in Ireland. The FBI has increased the reward to one million dollars.

Photograph altered in 2000

FBI TEN MOST WANTED
MURDER

ERIC ROBERT RUDOLPH
$1,000,000 REWARD

Maliciously damaged, by means of an explosive device, buildings and property affecting interstate commerce which resulted in death and injury

Date of photograph unknown

Date of photograph unknown

Date of sketch July 1998

ALIASES: Bob Randolph, Robert Randolph, Bob Rudolph, Eric Rudolph and Eric R. Rudolph

DESCRIPTION

DATE OF BIRTH: September 19, 1966
PLACE OF BIRTH: Merritt Island, Florida
HEIGHT: 5'11"
WEIGHT: 165 to 180 pounds
BUILD: Medium
OCCUPATIONS: Carpenter, roofer and handyman

SCARS AND MARKS: He has a noticeable scar on his chin.
HAIR: Brown
EYES: Blue
COMPLEXION: Fair
SEX: Male
NATIONALITY: American

CAUTION

Eric Robert Rudolph is charged in connection with the bombing of a health clinic in Birmingham, Alabama, in which a police officer was killed and a nurse critically wounded. He is also charged in connection with the fatal bombings at Centennial Olympic Park in downtown Atlanta, Georgia, the double bombings at the Sandy Springs Professional Office Building north of Atlanta, and the double bombings at the Otherside Lounge in Midtown, Atlanta. These bomb blasts injured more than 150 people. Rudolph is known to own firearms and to have targeted law enforcement.

CONSIDERED ARMED AND DANGEROUS

INTERNATIONAL CRIME ALERT
ERIC ROBERT RUDOLPH

Eric Robert Rudolph is charged in connection with the bombing of a health clinic in Birmingham, Alabama, in which a police officer was killed and a nurse critically wounded. A pickup truck registered to Eric Rudolph, was seen near the site of the bombing. A witness reportedly saw a man wearing a wig flee the area after the explosion and jump into the pickup truck. Four days later, dozens of federal agents searched the Appalachian Mountains of North Carolina for Rudolph, telling the press they believed he could help them locate the bomber of an abortion clinic. The man being sought was wanted as a witness and not as a suspect they said.

By the end of February 1998 however, Rudolphs status changed from a material witness in the case to the main suspect. The FBI solicited the help of hundreds of volunteer searchers and offered a $1 Million reward in their effort to find Rudolph in the rugged North Carolina Mountains.

Agents search storage shed rented in North Carolina by Eric Rudolph

Since Rudolph disappeared into the mountains in August, 1998 he has been hunted continuously by the FBI, ATF, and literally hundreds of volunteers, including a group led by former Green Beret Colonel James Bo Gritz, who vowed to turn Rudolph over to local authorities if he surrenders and not to federal agents. After more than a week of fruitless searching Gritz and his band of volunteers gave up the hunt. In October 1998 Federal Agents doubled to 200, the number of law officers searching the Appalachians for Rudolph.

November 25, 1998, FBI Director Louis Freeh visited with Federal Agents who were continuing the search For Rudolph. In June 1999, the size of the government force hunting him was reduced when 25 prison guards were recalled. This left the existing number of searchers at less than 100.

Bombed abortion clinic in Birmingham, Alabama

In addition to the health clinic, he is also charged in connection with the fatal bombings at Centennial Olympic Park in downtown Atlanta, Georgia, the double bombings at the Sandy Springs Professional Office Building north of Atlanta, and the double bombings at the Otherside lounge in midtown Atlanta. These bomb blasts injured more than 150 people.

The public is asked to revisit their photographs and videotapes taken during the Atlanta Olympics to determine if any of the photographs or videos contains footage, which may resemble Eric Robert Rudolph. He may be wearing khaki colored shorts, a dark T-shirt, dark ankle length boots, and lighter colored socks.

On March 20, 2002, after a nearly four year, more than $30 million manhunt, the FBI is scaling back its search for Rudolph. We are pretty much done, said Todd Letcher, who runs the Southeast Bomb Task Force. The task force has also finished compiling evidence to be turned over to a defense team should the case against Rudolph ever reach court. While Letcher said no final decision has been made, the fugitive investigation will probably be transferred to the FBIs field office in Charlotte, North Carolina.

Agents search house near where pickup truck was found

FBI TEN MOST WANTED
ARMED ROBBERY

VICTOR MANUEL GERENA
$400,000 REWARD

Bank robbery; unlawful flight to avoid prosecution – armed robbery; theft from interstate shipment

Photograph taken in 1983

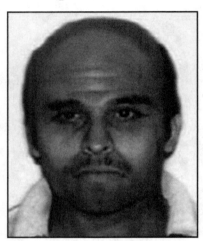

Age enhanced photo

ALIASES: Victor Ortiz and Victor M. Gerena Ortiz

DESCRIPTION

DATE OF BIRTH: June 24, 1958
PLACE OF BIRTH: New York, NY
HEIGHT: 5'6" to 5'7"
WEIGHT: 160 to 169 pounds
BUILD: Medium/Stocky
OCCUPATIONS: Machinist, security guard
COMPLEXION: Dark/Medium

SCARS AND MARKS: He has a one-inch scar and a mole on his right shoulder blade.
HAIR: Brown
EYES: Green
RACE: White
SEX: Male
NATIONALITY: American (Puerto Rican descent)

CAUTION

On September 12, 1983, a twenty- five-year-old security guard for the Wells Fargo armored car service takes two fellow employees hostage at the company's terminal in West Hartford, Connecticut. The hostages are handcuffed, blindfolded, and injected with an unknown substance that disables them for several hours. The assailant drives away in a rented vehicle with more than seven million dollars. The man wanted for this crime is Victor Manuel Gerena. He was recruited, trained, and directed to carry out the Wells Fargo robbery by a Puerto Rican terrorist group called the Macheteros (Machete Wielders).

CONSIDERED ARMED AND DANGEROUS

FBI TEN MOST WANTED
MURDER, DRUG CONSPIRACY

HOPETON ERIC BROWN
$50,000 REWARD

Drug conspiracy; carrying a weapon in relation to a drug-trafficking crime; murder in relation to a drug-trafficking crime; attempted murder of a witness

ALIASES: Anthony Brisco, Simon Plested, Devon Foster, Eric Brown, Omar Brown, Richard Omar Kennedy, Richard Omar Kennedy Sandokam, "Sando", "Angel", "Shawn"

DESCRIPTION

DATES OF BIRTH USED: September 26, 1974 / August 26, 1974	**SCARS AND MARKS:** Brown has a mole below his left eye and possibly a large scar on his chest.
PLACE OF BIRTH: Montego Bay, Jamaica	**HAIR:** Black
HEIGHT: 5'8"	**EYES:** Brown
WEIGHT: 175 pounds	**COMPLEXION:** Dark
BUILD: Medium	**RACE:** Black
OCCUPATION: Unknown	**SEX:** Male
COMPLEXION: Dark/Medium	**NATIONALITY:** Jamaican

REMARKS: Brown has been known to wear heavy gold jewelry. He has ties to Orlando, Tallahassee, Pensacola, and Miami, Florida; Minneapolis, Minnesota; Hartford, Connecticut; San Diego, California; London, England; and Jamaica. Brown may have travelled to Antigua, West Indies.

CAUTION

Hopeton Eric Brown is being sought in the United States for his alleged involvement in drug-related activities, as well as for the murder of a man and the attempted murder of a woman in March of 1997 in St. Paul, Minnesota. He is also wanted by authorities in Jamaica for allegedly committing two murders in Montego Bay in January of 2001.

CONSIDERED ARMED AND DANGEROUS

REWARDS FOR JUSTICE

Counter-Terrorism Rewards Program

U.S. OFFERS UP TO $25 MILLION FOR INFORMATION ABOUT TERRORISTS

The U.S. Department of State offers up to twenty five million dollars for information preventing, frustrating, or favorably resolving acts of international terrorism against United States persons or property, or leading to the arrest or conviction of terrorist criminals responsible for such acts, those aiding or abetting in the commission of such acts, or those conspiring or attempting to commit such acts.

PUBLIC-PRIVATE PARTNERSHIP

In 1990, the State Department forged a unique public-private partnership with the Air Transport Association of America and the Air Line Pilots Association, International, in which each organization pledged up to $1 million to supplement rewards paid by the U.S. Government for information that prevents a terrorist act against U.S. civil aviation, or leads to the arrest or conviction of any person who has committed such an act. The U.S. Government's standing reward offer of up to $25 million applies in all cases not addressed by the partnership agreement.

We Can Give You Twenty Five Million Reasons To Stop Terrorism.

INTERAGENCY REWARDS COMMITTEE

The Director of the Diplomatic Security Service, or his/her designee, chairs an interagency committee which reviews reward candidates and then recommends rewards to the Secretary of State. This committee serves as the forum for discussion of many aspects of the Program. The Interagency Rewards Committee, depending upon the incident under review, is comprised of representatives from the White House National Security Council staff, the Central Intelligence Agency, the Department of Justice, the Federal Bureau of Investigation, the Drug Enforcement Administration, the U.S. Marshals Service Witness Security Program, the Immigration and Naturalization Service, the Federal Aviation Administration, the Department of Energy, the Department of State, and others as appropriate.

EVERY GOVERNMENT AND EVERY CITIZEN

While the law governing the Rewards Program is aimed at terrorism directed against Americans, the United States shares information with other nations whose citizens are at risk. Every government and every citizen has a stake in bringing terrorists to justice and in preventing acts of terrorism.

Terrorists are violent criminals. They must be stopped.

Terrorism: Use of violence, or the threat of violence, to create a climate of fear in a given population. Terrorist violence targets ethnic or religious groups, governments, political parties, corporations, and media enterprises. Organizations that engage in acts of terror are almost always small in size and limited in resources compared to the populations and institutions they oppose. Through publicity and fear generated by their violence, they seek to magnify their influence and power to effect political change on either a local or an international scale.

"Terrorism," Microsoft® Encarta® Online Encyclopedia 2001

REWARDS FOR JUSTICE

MASS MURDER
$25,000,000 REWARD
WORLD TRADE CENTER AND THE PENTAGON

On September 11, 2001, terrorists hijacked four commercial airliners. Two of these were used to attack the New York World Trade Center Twin Towers and one was used to attack the Pentagon. The fourth airliner crashed into a field near Shanksville, PA. The death toll on the four airliners was 266 people. The death toll at the Pentagon is approximately 189 military and civilian personnel and the death toll in New York is approximately 3,000 people. The first flight, American Airlines Flight 11, smashed into the north tower of the Twin Towers at 8:45a.m. The second flight, United Airlines Flight 175, crashed into the south tower at 9:05a.m. The Pentagon was hit by American Airlines Flight 77 at 9:39a.m. American Airlines Flight 93 crashed before it reached its intended target.

Individuals providing information about these attacks may be eligible for a reward of up to $25 million, protection of identities and relocation with their families.

If you have any information and are overseas, contact the nearest US embassy or consulate; otherwise use the contact information below.

Rewards for Justice
P.O. Box 96781
Washington, D.C. 20522-0303, USA
Internet: mail@rewardsforjustice.net
Voice: 1-800-USREWARDS

ALL RESPONSES ARE KEPT STRICTLY CONFIDENTIAL

REWARDS FOR JUSTICE

MASS MURDER
$25,000,000 REWARD
PAN AM FLIGHT 103 BOMBING

On December 21, 1988, terrorists destroyed Pan American Flight 103. The terrorist bombing of Pan Am 103 over Scotland points to the global impact of terrorism. The plane carried 259 citizens from 30 nations, including the United States, when it was destroyed over Lockerbie, Scotland; another 11 persons perished on the ground.

Civilized people everywhere reacted with horror and disgust to this atrocity. Terrorist fanatics hold us all hostage to the fear that we or our children may be the next innocent victims. Civilized people can take a stand. And we must.

What might it take to prevent another senseless bloodbath, the further slaughter of innocent children, men and women? A tip to the authorities. A single anonymous call or letter to us.

Timely information has thwarted terrorist plots in the past. It can do so again. Whatever information, rumor or suspicion you pass on will be held in the strictest confidence.

Rewards for Justice
P.O. Box 96781
Washington, D.C. 20522-0303, USA
Internet: mail@rewardsforjustice.net
Voice: 1-800-USREWARDS

ALL RESPONSES ARE KEPT STRICTLY CONFIDENTIAL

REWARDS FOR JUSTICE

MASS MURDER
$5,000,000 REWARD
TERRORIST ATTACK ON U.S.S. COLE, ADEN, YEMEN

On October 12, 2000, terrorist in a boat attacked the USS Cole in the harbor at Aden, Yemen. This attack killed 17 sailors and wounded over 30 others. To bring to justice those responsible for this attack, the U.S. Government is offering a reward of up to $5 million for information leading to the arrest or conviction of those persons who committed or aided in the attack on the USS Cole.

The US Government has already paid millions of dollars to individuals who provided information that resulted in the arrest of someone who attempted or committed a terrorist act against US persons or property. Some of the individuals who provided such information have had their identities changed and been relocated with their families.

Individuals providing information may be eligible for a reward of up to $5 million, protection of identities, and relocation with their families. If you have information contact the nearest US embassy or consulate, or write:

Rewards for Justice
P.O. Box 96781
Washington, D.C. 20522-0303, USA
Internet: mail@rewardsforjustice.net
Voice: 1-800-USREWARDS

ALL RESPONSES ARE KEPT STRICTLY CONFIDENTIAL

REWARDS FOR JUSTICE

MASS MURDER

$5,000,000 REWARD

TWA FLIGHT 847 HIJACKING

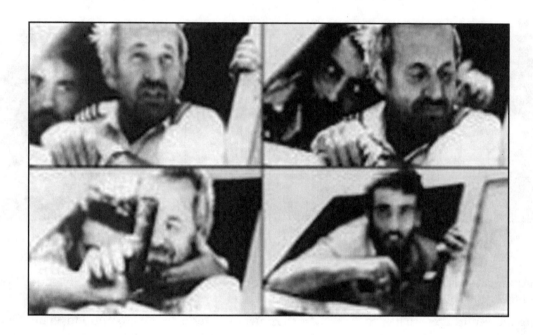

June 13, 1985: Terrorists hijack TWA Flight 847, killing Navy Diver Robert Stethem and dumping his body onto the tarmac. To bring these murderers to justice, the United States Government is offering a reward of up to $5 million. The money is available under a program to obtain information that helps punish those responsible for past international terrorist acts against U.S. persons or property and prevent future such acts.

Rewards for Justice
P.O. Box 96781
Washington, D.C. 20522-0303, USA
Internet: mail@rewardsforjustice.net
Voice: 1-800-USREWARDS
ALL RESPONSES ARE KEPT STRICTLY CONFIDENTIAL

REWARDS FOR JUSTICE

KIDNAP – MURDER

$5,000,000 REWARD

AMERICAN HOSTAGES IN LEBANON

William Higgins
Murdered 1989

Peter Kilburn
Murdered 1986

William Buckley
Murdered 1985

Three American hostages did not come back from Lebanon. Their agonizing captivity ended not in freedom, but in cold-blooded execution at the hands of their captors.

To bring their murderers to justice, the U.S. government is offering a reward of up to $5 million. The money is available under a program to obtain information that helps punish those responsible for past international terrorist acts against U.S. persons or property and prevent future such acts.

In the United States, call your local office of the Federal Bureau of Investigation or Diplomatic Security at 1-800-USREWARDS, or write to:If you have any information and are overseas, contact the nearest US embassy or consulate; otherwise use the contact information below.

Rewards for Justice
P.O. Box 96781
Washington, D.C. 20522-0303, USA
Internet: mail@rewardsforjustice.net
Voice: 1-800-USREWARDS

ALL RESPONSES ARE KEPT STRICTLY CONFIDENTIAL

REWARDS FOR JUSTICE

KARACHI, PAKISTAN: UTP MURDERS

$5,000,000 REWARD

AMERICAN HOSTAGES IN LEBANON

Ephrahim C. Egbu

William L. Jennings

Anwar Mirza

Tracy L. Ritchie

Joel B. Enlow

On the morning of November 12, 1997, Ephrahim C. Egbu, Joel B. Enlow, William L. Jennings, and Tracy L. Ritchie, employees of the Union Texas Petroleum Company (UTP) who were in Karachi on temporary assignment, were picked up from the Sheraton Hotel for a ride to UTP headquarters along the waterfront. As the station wagon in which they were traveling proceeded across the only bridge leading to the UTP office building, a red Honda Civic pulled in front and two gunmen jumped out. The gunmen fired into the UTP station wagon, brutally murdering the Pakistani driver, Anwar Mirza, and Messrs. Egbu, Enlow, Jennings and Ritchie.

The United States Department of State and the Diplomatic Security Service are offering a reward of up to $5 million for information or other assistance that leads to the arrest or conviction, in any country, of those responsible for this cowardly attack against civilians. The U.S. Government will also provide for the protection of identity and the possibility of relocation for persons who contribute such information and their families.

Persons wishing to report information about the murderers of the Union Texas Petroleum Company employees or other terrorist attacks or the planning of future terrorist attacks should contact the authorities or the nearest U.S. embassy or consulate. In the United States, call your local office of the Federal Bureau of Investigation or the Bureau of Diplomatic Security at 1-800-USREWARDS, or write to:

Rewards for Justice
P.O. Box 96781
Washington, D.C. 20522-0303, USA
Internet: mail@rewardsforjustice.net
Voice: 1-800-USREWARDS

ALL RESPONSES ARE KEPT STRICTLY CONFIDENTIAL

REWARDS FOR JUSTICE

KARACHI, PAKISTAN CONSULATE MURDERS
$5,000,000 REWARD
AMERICAN HOSTAGES IN LEBANON

On March 8, 1995 in Karachi, Pakistan, terrorists armed with automatic rifles murdered two American consulate employees and wounded a third as they traveled in the consulate shuttle bus. A reward of up to $5 million is being offered for information that leads to the arrest or conviction, in any country, of those responsible for this cowardly attack against unarmed American civilians. The U.S. Government will also provide for the protection of identity and the possibility of relocation for persons who contribute such information and their families. Persons wishing to report information about this terrorist attack on American consulate employees in Karachi or other terrorist attacks or the planning of future terrorist attacks should contact the authorities or the nearest U.S. embassy or consulate.In the United States, call your local office of the Federal Bureau of Investigation or the Bureau of Diplomatic Security at 1-800-USREWARDS, or write to:

Rewards for Justice
P.O. Box 96781
Washington, D.C. 20522-0303, USA
Internet: mail@rewardsforjustice.net
Voice: 1-800-USREWARDS

ALL RESPONSES ARE KEPT STRICTLY CONFIDENTIAL

REWARDS FOR JUSTICE

BOMBING OF KHOBAR TOWERS
$5,000,000 REWARD

Fourteen terrorists were indicted on June 21, 2001 for the brutal and cowardly terrorist attack on a multi-national peacekeeping force in Dhahran, Saudi Arabia that left 19 dead and hundreds injured. These peacekeepers were enforcing United Nations sanctions and the dead and injured included citizens from several nations. Peace in our time can only be assured in a world free from terrorism and the loss of innocent lives.

According to the indictment returned by a Federal Grand Jury in Alexandria, Virginia, nine of the fourteen are charged with 46 separate criminal counts including: conspiracy to kill Americans and employees of the United States, to use weapons of mass destruction, and to destroy U.S. property; bombing; and murder. The five others are each charged with five conspiracy counts. The indictment alleges that the conspiracy was driven by the motive to expel Americans from the Kingdom of Saudi Arabia.

The indictment charges Ahmad Al-Mughassil, also known as Abu Omran; Ali El-Hoorie also known as Ali Al-Houri; Hani Al-Sayegh; Ibrahim Al-Yacoub; Abdelkarim Al-Nasser; Mustafa Al-Qassab; Abdallah Al-Jarash; Hussein Al-Mughis; and the unidentified Lebanese, listed as "John Doe," with all five charges. Sa'ed Al-Bahar, Saleh Ramadan, Ali Al-Marhoun, Mustafa Al-Mu'alem and Fadel Al-Alawe are named in the five conspiracy counts.

Rewards for Justice, P.O. Box 96781, Washington, D.C. 20522-0303, USA
Internet: mail@rewardsforjustice.net
Voice: 1-800-USREWARDS

ALL RESPONSES ARE KEPT STRICTLY CONFIDENTIAL

REWARDS FOR JUSTICE

BOMBING OF WORLD TRADE CENTER
$25,000,000 REWARD
SIX INNOCENT PEOPLE MURDERED

WANTED

Abdul Rahmah Yasin

CAPTURED

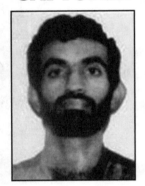

Ramzi Ahmed Yousef

At approximately 12 noon on February 26, 1993, a massive explosion rocked the World Trade Center in New York City, causing millions of dollars in damage. The terrorists who bombed the World Trade Center murdered six innocent people, injured over 1,000 others, and left terrified school children trapped for hours in a smoke-filled elevator.

If you have any information about the the World Trade Center bombing, or Abdul Rhamah Yasin, contact the nearest U. S. embassy or consulate. In the United States, call your local office of the Federal Bureau of Investigation or the Bureau of Diplomatic Security at 1-800-USREWARDS, or write to:

Rewards for Justice
P.O. Box 96781
Washington, D.C. 20522-0303, USA
Internet: mail@rewardsforjustice.net
Voice: 1-800-USREWARDS

ALL RESPONSES ARE KEPT STRICTLY CONFIDENTIAL

REWARDS FOR JUSTICE

BOMBING OF U.S. EMBASSIES
IN EAST AFRICA
$25,000,000 REWARD

On August 7, 1998, 224 innocent civilians were killed by terrorist bombs when they exploded at the U.S. embassies in Nairobi, Kenya and Dar es Salaam, Tanzania. These two cowardly attacks seriously wounded over 5,000 men, women and children. Civilized people everywhere reject such acts of random violence.

Usama Bin Laden, Muhammad Atef, Ayman Al Zawahiri, Mustafa Mohammed Fadhil, Fazul Abdullah Mohammed, Ahmed Khalfan Ghailani, Fahid Mohammed Ally Msalam , Sheikh Ahmed Salim Swedan, Abdullah Ahmed Abdullah, Saif Al-Adel, Anas Al-Liby, Ahmed Mohamed Hamed Ali, and Muhsin Musa Matwalli Atwah, and others already in custody are believed to be responsible for the bombings of the U.S. embassies in Tanzania and Kenya on August, 7, 1998. These terrorist attacks indiscriminately killed 224 innocent civilians and wounded over 5,000 others. These terrorist are believed to be part of an international criminal conspiracy headed by Usama Bin Laden. The U. S. Government is offering a reward for information leading to the arrest or conviction, in any country, of those people listed above.

A reward of up to $25 million may be paid to any person who furnishes such information. The reward is available under the Counter-Terrorism Rewards Program. This program is designed to protect innocent lives by punishing those responsible for past international terrorist acts against U.S. persons or property and preventing future such acts. The program provides for the protection of identity and the possibility of relocation for persons who contribute such information and their families. Persons wishing to report information about these bombings, or any other terrorist attack, should contact the nearest U.S. embassy or consulate. In the United States, call your local office of the Federal Bureau of Investigation or the Bureau of Diplomatic Security at 1-800-USREWARDS, or write to:

Rewards for Justice, P.O. Box 96781, Washington, D.C. 20522-0303, USA
Internet: mail@rewardsforjustice.net
Voice: 1-800-USREWARDS

ALL RESPONSES ARE KEPT STRICTLY CONFIDENTIAL

SPECIAL REWARD
Up to $2.5 Million

For information leading to the arrest and conviction of the individual(s) responsible for the mailing of letters containing anthrax to the New York Post, Tom Brokaw at NBC, Senator Tom Daschle and Senator Patrick Leahy.

AS A RESULT OF EXPOSURE TO ANTHRAX,
FIVE (5) PEOPLE HAVE DIED.

The person responsible for these deaths…
• Likely has a scientific background/work history which may include a specific familiarity with anthrax
• Has a specific level of comfort in and around the Trenton, NJ area due to present or prior association

Anyone having information, contact America's Most Wanted at 1-800-CRIME TV or the FBI via e-mail at amerithrax@fbi.gov

All information will be held in strict confidence. Reward payment will be made in accordance with the conditions of Postal Service Reward Notice 296, dated February 2000. Source of reward funds:

U.S. Postal Service and FBI $2,000,000; ADVO, Inc. $500,000.

Joint Press Release by FBI Newark and the United States Postal Inspection Service:

A nationally-coordinated criminal investigative effort, under the direction of FBI Washington Field Office Assistant Director Van Harp and Chief Postal Inspector Kenneth C. Weaver, involving the FBI and the United States Postal Inspection Service in Trenton, NJ; Washington, D.C.; Miami, FL; New York, NY; and Oxford, CT, continues to address the anthrax tainted letters which were postmarked in Trenton, NJ. To date, a total of five (5) innocent people have died as a result of their unsuspecting exposure to Anthrax.

In furtherance of this investigation, the United States Postal Service began delivery of a flyer which requests the continued assistance of the American public in this case. The initial delivery of this flyer was to postal customers of the Trenton, NJ area and to adjacent communities of Bucks County, PA. Additionally, the flyers will be distributed to New Jersey area pharmaceutical companies and transportation depots servicing the Trenton area.

These flyers contain a photograph of the four envelopes and information that may characterize the person(s) who prepared and mailed them. These envelopes are not standard business size, but are pre-stamped, smaller-sized envelopes measuring $6\frac{1}{4}$" x 3", and would have been sold at United States Post Offices and authorized retail outlets. The flyer also indicates that the person(s) responsible for the five deaths caused by the mailings is "likely to have a scientific background/ work history which may include a specific familiarity with anthrax." Also, "this individual has a comfort level in and around the Trenton, NJ area due to present or prior association."

The reward for information has been increased up to $2,500,000 for information leading to the arrest and conviction of the individual(s) responsible for mailing the four (4) Anthrax letters. $2,000,000 is being offered by the FBI and US Postal Service and $500,000 by ADVO, Inc.

This investigation in New Jersey is being conducted by a task force, composed of numerous federal, state, and local law enforcement agencies as well as public health agencies from all levels. The task force has received a tremendous amount of information from the general public. As a result of this outstanding response, thousands of leads have been vigorously followed to their logical conclusion.

The task force is continuing to request the public's assistance in this complex investigation which involves both public health concerns and a criminal investigation. We have reason to believe there are individuals who may have information pertinent to this investigation who have yet to come forward.

"Those responsible for the anthrax-tainted letters must be brought to justice," New Jersey Governor James E. McGreevey said. "To this end, I urge the citizens of New Jersey to cooperate fully with the FBI, Postal Service, and state and local law enforcement."

Information about suspicious person(s) or any other issue(s) deemed out of the ordinary concerning this investigation could be extremely important to the investigative team. Even if you think that your information is unimportant, or that someone else may have already reported what you know, please contact us immediately. Your call may be the one that provides us with the one piece of information needed to solve this case. Please, do not assume that your information has already been provided. "The mailings on September 18, 2001 and October 9, 2001 were an unprecedented attack on our nation's mail system. Although many of the initial investigative resources were concentrated in New Jersey, we continue to broaden the scope of the investigation and try different techniques, such as this flyer, to bring this to a successful conclusion," stated Chief Postal Inspector Kenneth C. Weaver.

"We thank the individuals who have reached out and provided information since the inception and hope that these flyers and the newly augmented reward will encourage others to contact us," said FBI Assistant Director Van Harp.

Call 1-800-CRIME TV (1-800-274-6388) or go to amerithrax@ fbi.gov on the web.

22 MOST WANTED TERRORISTS

To date, these are the 22 Most Wanted Terrorists by the Federal Bureau of Investigation for numerous acts of terrorism worldwide from 1985 to the most recent Attack on America on September 11, 2001. Under the Rewards for Justice Program up to $25 million is offered for information that prevents, frustrates, or favorably resolves acts of international terrorism against U.S. interests worldwide or leads to the arrest or conviction in any country of an individual for the commission of such an act.

Usama Bin Laden

Ayman Al-Zawahiri

Abdelkarim Hussein Mohamed Al-Nasser

Abdullah Ahmed Abdullah

Mushin Musa Matwalli Atwah

Ali Atwa

Anas Al-Liby

Ahmed Khalfan Ghailani

Hassan Izz-Al-Din

Ahmed Mohammed Hamed Ali

Fazul Abdullah Mohammed

Imad Mugniyah

Mustafa Mohamed Fadhil

Sheikh Ahmed Salim Swedan

Abdul Rahman Yasin

Fahid Mohammed Ally Msalam

Ahmad Ibrahim Al-Mughassil

Khalid Shaikh Mohammed

Muhammad Atef

Ali Saed Bin Ali El-Hoorie

Saif Al-Adel

Ibrahim Salih Mohammed Al-Yacoub

WANTED
TERRORISM, MURDER

AYMAN AL-ZAWAHIRI
$25,000,000 REWARD

Offenses: Crimes against property, firearms ammunitions, firearms ammunitions illegal possession, forgery, murder, murder conspiracy, terrorism, terrorism illegal possession

WANTED BY THE FBI

ALIASES: Abu Muhammad, Abu Fatima, Muhammad Ibrahim, Abu Abdallah, Abu al-Mu'iz, The Doctor, The Teacher, Nur, Ustaz, Abu Mohammed, Abu Mohammed Nur al-Deen, Abdel Muaz, Dr. Ayman al Zawahiri

DESCRIPTION

DATE OF BIRTH:	September 19, 1966	**HAIR:**	Brown/Black
PLACE OF BIRTH:	Egypt	**EYES:**	Brown
HEIGHT:	Unknown	**COMPLEXION:**	Fair
WEIGHT:	Unknown	**SEX:**	Male
BUILD:	Medium	**NATIONALITY:**	Egyptian

Ayman Al Zawahiri is a physician and the founder of the Egyptian Islamic Jihad. This organization opposes the secular Egyptian Government and seeks its overthrow through violent means. Al Zawahiri is believed to now serve as an advisor and doctor to Usama Bin Laden and is currently thought to be in Afghanistan. He has been indicted for his alleged role in the August 7, 1998, bombings of the U.S. Embassies in Dar es Salaam, Tanzania and Nairobi, Kenya. Indicted for: murder of U.S. nationals outside the United States; conspiracy to murder U.S. nationals outside the United States; attack on a Federal Facility resulting in death. Usama Bin Laden, Muhammad Atef, Ayman Al Zawahiri, Mustafa Mohammed Fadhil, Fazul Abdullah Mohammed, Ahmed Khalfan Ghailani, Fahid Mohammed Ally Msalam, Sheikh Ahmed Salim Swedan, Abdullah Ahmed Abdullah, Saif Al-Adel, Anas Al-Liby, Ahmed Mohamed Hamed Ali, and Muhsin Musa Matwalli Atwah, and others already in custody are believed to be responsible for the bombings of the U.S. embassies in Tanzania and Kenya on August, 7, 1998. These terrorist attacks indiscriminately killed 224 innocent civilians and wounded over 5,000 others. These terrorist are believed to be part of an international criminal conspiracy headed by Usama Bin Laden. The U. S. Government is offering a reward for information leading to the arrest or conviction, in any country, of those people listed above.

WANTED
TERRORISM, MURDER

ABDELKARIM HUSSEIN MOHAMED AL-NASSER
$25,000,000 REWARD

CONSPIRACY TO KILL U.S. NATIONALS; CONSPIRACY TO MURDER U.S. EMPLOYEES; CONSPIRACY TO USE WEAPONS OF MASS DESTRUCTION AGAINST U.S. NATIONALS; CONSPIRACY TO DESTROY PROPERTY OF THE U. S.; CONSPIRACY TO ATTACK NATIONAL DEFENSE UTILITIES; BOMBING RESULTING IN DEATH; USE OF WEAPONS OF MASS DESTRUCTION AGAINST U.S. NATIONALS; MURDER WHILE USING DESTRUCTIVE DEVICE DURING A CRIME OF VIOLENCE; MURDER OF FEDERAL EMPLOYEES; ATTEMPTED MURDER OF FEDERAL EMPLOYEES

WANTED BY THE FBI

ALIASES: None known

DESCRIPTION

DATE OF BIRTH: Unknown	**HAIR:** Black
PLACE OF BIRTH: Al Ihsa, Saudi Arabia	**EYES:** Brown
HEIGHT: 5'8"	**COMPLEXION:** Olive
WEIGHT: 170 lbs.	**SEX:** Male
BUILD: Unknown	**CITIZENSHIP:** Saudi Arabian
LANGUAGES: Arabic, Farsi	

CAUTION

Abdelkarim Hussein Mohamed Al-Nasser has been indicted in the Eastern District of Virginia for the June 25, 1996, bombing of the Khobar Towers military housing complex in Dhahran, Kingdom of Saudi Arabia. The Rewards For Justice Program, United States Department of State, is offering a reward of up to $25 million for information leading directly to the apprehension or indictment of Abdelkarim Hussein Mohamed Al-Nasser.

WANTED
TERRORISM, MURDER

ABDULLAH AHMED ABDULLAH
$25,000,000 REWARD

MURDER OF U.S. NATIONALS OUTSIDE THE UNITED STATES; CONSPIRACY TO MURDER U.S. NATIONALS OUTSIDE THE UNITED STATES; ATTACK ON A FEDERAL FACILITY RESULTING IN DEATH; CONSPIRACY TO KILL U.S. NATIONALS, TO MURDER, TO DESTROY BUILDINGS AND PROPERTY OF THE UNITED STATES, AND TO DESTROY THE NATIONAL DEFENSE UTILITIES OF THE UNITED STATES

WANTED BY THE FBI

ALIASES: Abu Mohamed Al-Masri, Saleh, Abu Mariam

DESCRIPTION

DATE OF BIRTH: Approximately 1963	**SCARS AND MARKS:** Abdullah has a scar on the right side of his lower lip.
PLACE OF BIRTH: Egypt	
HEIGHT: Approximately 5'8"	**HAIR:** Black
WEIGHT: Unknown	**EYES:** Brown
BUILD: Medium	**COMPLEXION:** Olive
LANGUAGES: Arabic	**SEX:** Male
	CITIZENSHIP: Saudi Arabian

REMARKS: Abdullah fled Nairobi, Kenya on August 6, 1998 and went to Karachi, Pakistan. He is believed to currently be in Afghanistan. He may wear a mustache.

CAUTION

Abdullah Ahmed Abdullah has been indicted for his alleged involvement in the August 7, 1998, bombings of the United States Embassies in Dar es Salaam, Tanzania, and Nairobi, Kenya. The Rewards For Justice Program, United States Department of State, is offering a reward of up to $25 million for information leading directly to the apprehension or conviction of Abdullah Ahmed Abdullah.

WANTED
TERRORISM

MUHSIN MUSA MATWALLI ATWAH
$25,000,000 REWARD

CONSPIRACY TO KILL UNITED STATES NATIONALS, TO MURDER, TO DESTROY BUILDINGS AND PROPERTY OF THE UNITED STATES, AND TO DESTROY NATIONAL DEFENSE UTILITIES OF THE UNITED STATES

WANTED BY THE FBI

ALIASES: Abdul Rahman, Abdul Rahman Al-Muhajir, Abdel Rahman, Mohammed K.A. Al-Namer

DESCRIPTION

DATE OF BIRTH: June 19, 1964	**SCARS AND MARKS:** None known
PLACE OF BIRTH: Egypt	**HAIR:** Dark, graying
HEIGHT: Approximately 5'3" to 5'7"	**EYES:** Dark
WEIGHT: Unknown	**COMPLEXION:** Olive
BUILD: Medium	**SEX:** Male
LANGUAGES: Arabic	**CITIZENSHIP:** Egyptian

CAUTION

Muhsin Musa Matwalli Atwah is wanted in connection with the August 7, 1998, bombings of the United States Embassies in Dar es Salaam, Tanzania, and Nairobi, Kenya. The Rewards For Justice Program, United States Department of State, is offering a reward of up to $25 million for information leading directly to the apprehension and/or conviction of Muhsin Musa Matwalli Atwah.

WANTED
TERRORISM, MURDER

ALI ATWA
$25,000,000 REWARD

CONSPIRACY TO COMMIT AIRCRAFT PIRACY, TO COMMIT HOSTAGE TAKING, TO COMMIT AIR PIRACY RESULTING IN MURDER, TO INTERFERE WITH A FLIGHT CREW, TO PLACE A DESTRUCTIVE DEVICE ABOARD AN AIRCRAFT, TO HAVE EXPLOSIVE DEVICES ABOUT THE PERSON ON AN AIRCRAFT, AND TO ASSAULT PASSENGERS AND CREW; AIR PIRACY RESULTING IN MURDER; AIR PIRACY; HOSTAGE TAKING; INTERFERENCE WITH FLIGHT CREW; AND PLACING EXPLOSIVES ABOARD AIRCRAFT; PLACING DESTRUCTIVE DEVICES ABOARD AIRCRAFT; ASSAULT ABOARD AIRCRAFT WITH INTENT TO HIJACK WITH A DANGEROUS WEAPON AND RESULTING IN SERIOUS BODILY INJURY; AIDING AND ABETTING

WANTED BY THE FBI

ALIASES: Ammar Mansour Bouslim, Hassan Rostom Salim

DESCRIPTION

DATE OF BIRTH: Approximately 1960	SCARS AND MARKS: None known
PLACE OF BIRTH: Lebanon	HAIR: Unknown
HEIGHT: 5'8"	EYES: Brown
WEIGHT: Unknown	COMPLEXION: Olive
BUILD: Medium	SEX: Male
LANGUAGES: Arabic	CITIZENSHIP: Lebanese

REMARKS: Atwa is an alleged member of the terrorist organization, Lebanese Hizballah. He is thought to be in Lebanon.

CAUTION

Ali Atwa was indicted for his role and participation in the June 14, 1985, hijacking of a commercial airliner which resulted in the assault on various passengers and crew members, and the murder of one U.S. citizen. The Rewards For Justice Program, United States Department of State, is offering a reward of up to $25 million for information leading directly to the apprehension and/or conviction of Ali Atwa.

WANTED
TERRORISM

ANAS AL-LIBY
$25,000,000 REWARD

CONSPIRACY TO KILL U.S. NATIONALS, TO MURDER, TO DESTROY BUILDINGS AND PROPERTY OF THE UNITED STATES, AND TO DESTROY THE NATIONAL DEFENSE UTILITIES OF THE UNITED STATES

WANTED BY THE FBI

ALIASES: Anas Al-Sabai, Anas Al-Libi, Nazih Al-Raghie, Nazih Abdul Hamed Al-Raghie

DESCRIPTION

DATES OF BIRTH USED: March 30, 1964; May 14, 1964	**SCARS AND MARKS:** Al-Liby has a scar on the left side of his face.
PLACE OF BIRTH: Tripoli, Libya	**HAIR:** Dark
HEIGHT: 5'10" to 6'2"	**EYES:** Dark
WEIGHT: Unknown	**COMPLEXION:** Olive
BUILD: Medium	**SEX:** Male
LANGUAGES: Arabic, English	**CITIZENSHIP:** Libyan

REMARKS: Al-Liby recently lived in the United Kingdom, where he has political asylum. He is believed to currently be in Afghanistan. Al-Liby usually wears a full beard.

CAUTION

Anas Al-Liby is wanted in connection with the August 7, 1998, bombings of the United States Embassies in Dar es Salaam, Tanzania, and Nairobi, Kenya. The Rewards For Justice Program, United States Department of State, is offering a reward of up to $25 million for information leading directly to the apprehension or conviction of Anas Al-Liby.

WANTED
TERRORISM, MURDER

AHMED KHALFAN GHAILANI
$25,000,000 REWARD

MURDER OF U.S. NATIONALS OUTSIDE THE UNITED STATES; CONSPIRACY TO MURDER U.S. NATIONALS OUTSIDE THE UNITED STATES; ATTACK ON A FEDERAL FACILITY RESULTING IN DEATH

WANTED BY THE FBI

ALIASES: Ahmad Khalafan Ghilani, Ahmed Khalfan Ahmed, Abubakar K. Ahmed, Abubakary K. Ahmed, Abubakar Ahmed, Abu Bakr Ahmad, A. Ahmed, Ahmed Khalfan, Ahmed Khalfan Ali, Abubakar Khalfan Ahmed, Ahmed Ghailani, Ahmad Al Tanzani, Abu Khabar, Abu Bakr, Abubakary Khalfan Ahmed Ghailani, Mahafudh Abubakar Ahmed Abdallah Hussein, Shariff Omar Mohammed, "Foopie", "Fupi", "Ahmed the Tanzanian"

DESCRIPTION

DATES OF BIRTH USED: March 14, 1974; April 13, 1974; April 14, 1974; August 1, 1970	**SCARS AND MARKS:** None known
PLACE OF BIRTH: Zanzibar, Tanzania	**HAIR:** Black
HEIGHT: 5'3" to 5'4"	**EYES:** Brown
WEIGHT: 150 lbs	**COMPLEXION:** Dark
BUILD: Unknown	**SEX:** Male
LANGUAGE: Swahili	**CITIZENSHIP:** Tanzanian

CAUTION

Ahmed Ghailani was indicted in the Southern District of New York, on December 16, 1998, for his alleged involvement in the August 7, 1998, bombings of the United States Embassies in Dar es Salaam, Tanzania, and Nairobi, Kenya. The Rewards For Justice Program, United States Department of State, is offering a reward of up to $25 million for information leading directly to the apprehension or conviction of Ahmed Ghailani.

WANTED
TERRORISM, MURDER

HASSAN IZZ-AL-DIN
$25,000,000 REWARD

CONSPIRACY TO COMMIT AIRCRAFT PIRACY, TO COMMIT HOSTAGE TAKING, TO COMMIT AIR PIRACY RESULTING IN MURDER, TO INTERFERE WITH A FLIGHT CREW, TO PLACE A DESTRUCTIVE DEVICE ABOARD AN AIRCRAFT, TO HAVE EXPLOSIVE DEVICES ABOUT THE PERSON ON AN AIRCRAFT, AND TO ASSAULT PASSENGERS AND CREW; AIR PIRACY RESULTING IN MURDER; AIR PIRACY; HOSTAGE TAKING; INTERFERENCE WITH FLIGHT CREW; AND PLACING EXPLOSIVES ABOARD AIRCRAFT; PLACING DESTRUCTIVE DEVICES ABOARD AIRCRAFT; ASSAULT ABOARD AIRCRAFT WITH INTENT TO HIJACK WITH A DANGEROUS WEAPON AND RESULTING IN SERIOUS BODILY INJURY; AIDING AND ABETTING

WANTED BY THE FBI

ALIASES: Ahmed Garbaya, Samir Salwwan, Sa-id

DESCRIPTION

DATE OF BIRTH USED: 1963	**SCARS AND MARKS:** None known
PLACE OF BIRTH: Lebanon	**HAIR:** Black
HEIGHT: 5'9" to 5'11"	**EYES:** Black
WEIGHT: 145 to 150 pounds	**SEX:** Male
BUILD: Slender	**CITIZENSHIP:** Lebanese
LANGUAGES: Arabic	

REMARKS: Izz-Al-Din is an alleged member of the terrorist organization, Lebanese Hizballah. He is thought to be in Lebanon.

CAUTION

Hasan Izz-Al-Din was indicted for his role in planning and participation in the June 14, 1985, hijacking of a commercial airliner which resulted in the assault on various passengers and crew members, and the murder of one U.S. citizen. The Rewards For Justice Program, United States Department of State, is offering a reward of up to $25 million for information leading directly to the apprehension and/or conviction of Hasan Izz-Al-Din.

WANTED
TERRORISM

AHMED MOHAMMED HAMED ALI
$25,000,000 REWARD

CONSPIRACY TO KILL UNITED STATES NATIONALS, TO MURDER, TO DESTROY BUILDINGS AND PROPERTY OF THE UNITED STATES, AND TO DESTROY NATIONAL DEFENSE UTILITIES OF THE UNITED STATES

WANTED BY THE FBI

ALIASES: Shuaib, Abu Islam Al-Surir, Ahmed Ahmed, Ahmed The Egyptian, Ahmed Hemed, Hamed Ali, Ahmed Shieb, Abu Islam, Ahmed Mohammed Ali, Ahmed Hamed, Ahmed Mohammed Abdurehman, Abu Khadiijah, Abu Fatima, Ahmad Al-Masri

DESCRIPTION

DATE OF BIRTH: Approximately 1965	**SCARS AND MARKS:** None known
PLACE OF BIRTH: Egypt	**HAIR:** Dark
HEIGHT: Approximately 5'8"	**EYES:** Dark
WEIGHT: Unknown	**COMPLEXION:** Olive
BUILD: Medium	**SEX:** Male
LANGUAGES: Arabic	**CITIZENSHIP:** Egyptian

REMARKS: Ali may have formal training in agriculture and may have worked in this field. He lived in Kenya until fleeing that country on August 2, 1998, to Karachi, Pakistan. He is believed to currently be in Afghanistan.

CAUTION

Ahmed Mohammed Hamed Ali is wanted in connection with the August 7, 1998, bombings of the United States Embassies in Dar es Salaam, Tanzania, and Nairobi, Kenya. The Rewards For Justice Program, United States Department of State, is offering a reward of up to $25 million for information leading directly to the apprehension and/or conviction of Ahmed Mohammed Hamed Ali.

WANTED
TERRORISM, MURDER

FAZUL ABDULLAH MOHAMMED
$25,000,000 REWARD

MURDER OF U.S. NATIONALS OUTSIDE THE UNITED STATES; CONSPIRACY TO
MURDER U.S. NATIONALS OUTSIDE THE UNITED STATES; ATTACK ON A
FEDERAL FACILITY RESULTING IN DEATH

WANTED BY THE FBI

ALIASES: Abdallah Fazul, Abdalla Fazul, Abdallah Mohammed Fazul, Fazul Abdilahi Mohammed,
Fazul Adballah, Fazul Abdalla, Fazul Mohammed, Haroon, Harun, Haroon Fazul, Harun Fazul,
Fadil Abdallah Muhamad, Fadhil Haroun, Abu Seif Al Sudani, Abu Aisha, Abu Luqman, Fadel
Abdallah Mohammed Ali, Fouad Mohammed

DESCRIPTION

DATES OF BIRTH USED: August 25, 1972; December 25, 1974; February 25, 1974	**LANGUAGES:** French, Swahili, Arabic, English, Comoran
PLACE OF BIRTH: Moroni, Comoros Islands	**HAIR:** Black
HEIGHT: Approximately 5'6" to 5'8"	**EYES:** Brown
WEIGHT: 120 to 140 pounds	**COMPLEXION:** Dark
BUILD: Medium	**SEX:** Male
SCARS AND MARKS: None known	**CITIZENSHIP:** Comoros, Kenyan

REMARKS: Mohammed likes to wear baseball caps and tends to dress casually. He is very good with computers.

CAUTION

Fazul Abdullah Mohammed was indicted on September 17, 1998, in the Southern District of New York, for his alleged involvement in the bombings of the United States Embassies in Dar es Salaam, Tanzania, and Nairobi, Kenya, on August 7, 1998. The Rewards For Justice Program, United States Department of State, is offering a reward of up to $25 million for information leading directly to the apprehension or conviction of Fazul Abdullah Mohammed.

WANTED
TERRORISM, MURDER

IMAD FAYEZ MUGNIYAH
$25,000,000 REWARD

CONSPIRACY TO COMMIT AIRCRAFT PIRACY, TO COMMIT HOSTAGE TAKING, TO COMMIT AIR PIRACY RESULTING IN MURDER, TO INTERFERE WITH A FLIGHT CREW, TO PLACE A DESTRUCTIVE DEVICE ABOARD AN AIRCRAFT, TO HAVE EXPLOSIVE DEVICES ABOUT THE PERSON ON AN AIRCRAFT, AND TO ASSAULT PASSENGERS AND CREW; AIR PIRACY RESULTING IN MURDER; AIR PIRACY; HOSTAGE TAKING; INTERFERENCE WITH FLIGHT CREW; AND PLACING EXPLOSIVES ABOARD AIRCRAFT; PLACING DESTRUCTIVE DEVICE ABOARD AIRCRAFT; ASSAULT ABOARD AIRCRAFT WITH INTENT TO HIJACK WITH A DANGEROUS WEAPON AND RESULTING IN SERIOUS BODILY INJURY; AIDING AND ABETTING

WANTED BY THE FBI

ALIAS: Hajj

DESCRIPTION

DATE OF BIRTH: 1962	SCARS AND MARKS: None known
PLACE OF BIRTH: Lebanon	HAIR: Brown
HEIGHT: 5'7"	EYES: Unknown
WEIGHT: 145 to 150 pounds	COMPLEXION: Olive
BUILD: Medium	SEX: Male
LANGUAGES: Arabic	CITIZENSHIP: Lebanese

REMARKS: Mugniyah is the alleged head of the security apparatus for the terrorist organization, Lebanese Hizballah. He is thought to be in Lebanon.

CAUTION

Imad Fayez Mugniyah was indicted for his role in planning and participation in the June 14, 1985, hijacking of a commercial airliner which resulted in the assault on various passengers and crew members, and the murder of one U.S. citizen. The Rewards For Justice Program, United States Department of State, is offering a reward of up to $25 million for information leading directly to the apprehension and/or conviction of Imad Fayez Mugniyah.

WANTED
TERRORISM, MURDER

MUSTAFA MOHAMED FADHIL
$25,000,000 REWARD

MURDER OF U.S. NATIONALS OUTSIDE THE UNITED STATES; CONSPIRACY TO MURDER
U.S. NATIONALS OUTSIDE THE UNITED STATES; ATTACK ON A FEDERAL FACILITY
RESULTING IN DEATH

WANTED BY THE FBI

ALIASES: Moustafa Ali Elbishy, Mustafa Mohammed, Mustafa Fazul, Hussein, Hassan Ali,
Mustafa Muhamad Fadil, Abd Al Wakil Al Masri, Abu Anis, Abu Yussrr, Hassan Ali, Nu Man,
Khalid, Abu Jihad, Abu Jihad al-Nubi

DESCRIPTION

DATE OF BIRTH: June 23, 1976	**SCARS AND MARKS:** None known
PLACE OF BIRTH: Cairo, Egypt	**HAIR:** Black, short and curly
HEIGHT: 5'3" to 5'5"	**EYES:** Brown
WEIGHT: 120 to 140 pounds	**COMPLEXION:** Olive
BUILD: Medium	**SEX:** Male
LANGUAGES: Arabic, Swahili, reads English	**CITIZENSHIP:** Egyptian, Kenyan

CAUTION

Mustafa Mohamed Fadhil was indicted in the Southern District of New York, on December 16, 1998, for his alleged involvement in the August 7, 1998, bombings of the U.S. Embassies in Dar es Salaam, Tanzania, and Nairobi, Kenya, and for conspiring to kill U.S. nationals. The Rewards For Justice Program, United States Department of State, is offering a reward of up to $25 million for information leading directly to the apprehension or conviction of Mustafa Mohamed Fadhil.

WANTED

TERRORISM, MURDER

SHEIKH AHMED SALIM SWEDAN
$25,000,000 REWARD

MURDER OF U.S. NATIONALS OUTSIDE THE UNITED STATES; CONSPIRACY TO MURDER
U.S. NATIONALS OUTSIDE THE UNITED STATES; ATTACK ON A FEDERAL FACILITY
RESULTING IN DEATH

WANTED BY THE FBI

ALIASES: Sheikh Ahmad Salem Suweidan, Sheikh Ahmed Salem Swedan, Sheikh Swedan, Sheikh
Bahamadi, Ahmed Ally, Bahamad, Sheik Bahamad, Ahmed the Tall

DESCRIPTION

DATES OF BIRTH USED: April 9, 1969; April 9, 1960	**SCARS AND MARKS:** None known
PLACE OF BIRTH: Mombasa, Kenya	**HAIR:** Black
HEIGHT: 5'8" to 6'0"	**EYES:** Brown
WEIGHT: 175 pounds	**COMPLEXION:** Dark
BUILD: Unknown	**SEX:** Male
LANGUAGES: Arabic, Swahili, English	**CITIZENSHIP:** Kenyan

REMARKS: Swedan sometimes wears a light beard or moustache and has, in the past, managed a trucking
business in Kenya.

CAUTION

Sheikh Ahmed Salim Swedan was indicted on December 16, 1998, in the Southern District of New York, for his
alleged involvement in the August 7, 1998, bombings of the United States Embassies in Dar es Salaam, Tanzania, and
Nairobi, Kenya, and for conspiring to kill U.S. nationals. The Rewards For Justice Program, United States
Department of State, is offering a reward of up to $25 million for information leading directly to the apprehension
or conviction of Sheikh Ahmed Salim Swedan.

WANTED
TERRORISM

ABDUL RAHMAN YASIN
$25,000,000 REWARD

DAMAGE BY MEANS OF FIRE OR AN EXPLOSIVE; DAMAGE BY MEANS OF FIRE OR AN EXPLOSIVE TO U.S. PROPERTY; TRANSPORT IN INTERSTATE COMMERCE OF AN EXPLOSIVE; DESTRUCTION OF MOTOR VEHICLES OR MOTOR VEHICLE FACILITIES; CONSPIRACY TO COMMIT OFFENSE OR DEFRAUD THE U.S.; AIDING AND ABETTING; PENALTY OF DEATH OR LIFE IMPRISONMENT WHEN DEATH RESULTS; ASSAULT OF A FEDERAL OFFICER IN THE LINE OF DUTY; COMMISSION OF A CRIME OF VIOLENCE THROUGH THE USE OF A DEADLY WEAPON OR DEVICE

WANTED BY THE FBI

ALIASES: Abdul Rahman Said Yasin, Aboud Yasin, Abdul Rahman S. Taha, Abdul Rahman S. Taher

DESCRIPTION

DATE OF BIRTH: Approximately 1963
PLACE OF BIRTH: Bloomington, Indiana
HEIGHT: 5'10"
WEIGHT: 180 pounds
BUILD: Unknown
LANGUAGES: Unknown

SCARS AND MARKS: Yasin possibly has a chemical burn scar on his right thigh.
HAIR: Black
EYES: Brown
COMPLEXION: Olive
SEX: Male
CITIZENSHIP: American

REMARKS: Yasin is an epileptic.

CAUTION

Abdul Rahman Yasin is wanted for his alleged participation in the terrorist bombing of the World Trade Center, New York City, on February 26, 1993, which resulted in six deaths, the wounding of numerous individuals, and the significant destruction of property and commerce. The Rewards For Justice Program, United States Department of State, is offering a reward of up to $25 million for information leading directly to the apprehension or conviction of Abdul Rahman Yasin.

WANTED
TERRORISM, MURDER

FAHID MOHAMMED ALLY MSALAM
$25,000,000 REWARD

MURDER OF U.S. NATIONALS OUTSIDE THE UNITED STATES; CONSPIRACY TO MURDER U.S. NATIONALS OUTSIDE THE UNITED STATES; ATTACK ON A FEDERAL FACILITY RESULTING IN DEATH

WANTED BY THE FBI

ALIASES: Fahid Mohammed Ally, Fahid Mohammed Ali Musalaam, Fahid Mohammed Ali Msalam, Fahid Muhamad Ali Salem, Mohammed Ally Msalam, Usama Al-Kini, Fahad Ally Msalam

DESCRIPTION

DATE OF BIRTH: February 19, 1976	**SCARS AND MARKS:** None known
PLACE OF BIRTH: Mombasa, Kenya	**HAIR:** Black, curly
HEIGHT: 5'6" to 5'8"	**EYES:** Brown
WEIGHT: 160 to 170 pounds	**COMPLEXION:** Olive
BUILD: Unknown	**SEX:** Male
LANGUAGES: Arabic, Swahili, English	**CITIZENSHIP:** Kenyan

REMARKS: Msalam sometimes wears a light beard or moustache and has, in the past, worked as a clothing vendor

CAUTION

Fahid Msalam was indicted on December 16, 1998, in the Southern District of New York, for his alleged involvement in the August 7, 1998, bombings of the United States Embassies in Dar es Salaam, Tanzania, and Nairobi, Kenya, and for conspiring to kill U.S. nationals. The Rewards For Justice Program, United States Department of State, is offering a reward of up to $25 million for information leading directly to the apprehension or conviction of Fahid Mohammed Ally Msalam.

WANTED
TERRORISM, MURDER

AHMAD IBRAHIM AL-MUGHASSIL
$25,000,000 REWARD

CONSPIRACY TO KILL U.S. NATIONALS; CONSPIRACY TO MURDER U.S. EMPLOYEES; CONSPIRACY TO USE WEAPONS OF MASS DESTRUCTION AGAINST U.S. NATIONALS; CONSPIRACY TO DESTROY PROPERTY OF THE U. S.; CONSPIRACY TO ATTACK NATIONAL DEFENSE UTILITIES; BOMBING RESULTING IN DEATH; USE OF WEAPONS OF MASS DESTRUCTION AGAINST U.S. NATIONALS; MURDER WHILE USING DESTRUCTIVE DEVICE DURING A CRIME OF VIOLENCE; MURDER OF FEDERAL EMPLOYEES; ATTEMPTED MURDER OF FEDERAL EMPLOYEES

WANTED BY THE FBI

ALIASES: Abu Omran

DESCRIPTION

DATE OF BIRTH: June 26, 1967	**SCARS AND MARKS:** None known.
PLACE OF BIRTH: Qatif - Bab Al Shamal, Saudi Arabia	**HAIR:** Black
HEIGHT: 5'4"	**EYES:** Brown
WEIGHT: 145 pounds	**COMPLEXION:** Olive
BUILD: Medium	**SEX:** Male
LANGUAGES: Arabic, Farsi	**CITIZENSHIP:** Saudi Arabian

CAUTION

Ahmad Ibrahim Al-Mughassil has been indicted in the Eastern District of Virginia for the June 25, 1996, bombing of the Khobar Towers military housing complex in Dhahran, Kingdom of Saudi Arabia. The Rewards For Justice Program, United States Department of State, is offering a reward of up to $25 million for information leading directly to the apprehension or indictment of Ahmad Ibrahim Al-Mughassil.

WANTED
TERRORISM

KHALID SHAIKH MOHAMMED
$25,000,000 REWARD

CONSPIRACY TO KILL NATIONALS OF THE UNITED STATES

WANTED BY THE FBI

ALIASES: Ashraf Refaat Nabith Henin, Khalid Adbul Wadood, Salem Ali, Fahd Bin Adballah Bin Khalid

DESCRIPTION

DATES OF BIRTH USED: April 14, 1965; March 1, 1964	**SCARS AND MARKS:** None known
PLACE OF BIRTH: Kuwait	**HAIR:** Black
HEIGHT: Approximately 5'8"	**EYES:** Brown
WEIGHT: Slightly Overweight	**COMPLEXION:** Olive
BUILD: Medium	**SEX:** Male
LANGUAGES: Unknown	**CITIZENSHIP:** Kuwaiti

REMARKS: Mohammed is known to wear either a full beard or a trimmed beard, or he may be clean shaven. He has been known to wear glasses.

CAUTION

Khalid Shaikh Mohammed is wanted for his alleged involvement in a conspiracy plot, based in Manila, The Philippines, to bomb commercial United States airliners flying routes to the United States from Southeast Asia in January of 1995. He was indicted in the Southern District of New York in January of 1996. The Rewards For Justice Program, United States Department of State, is offering a reward of up to $25 million for information leading directly to the apprehension or conviction of Khalid Shaikh Mohammed.

WANTED
TERRORISM, MURDER

MUHAMMED ATEF
$25,000,000 REWARD

MURDER OF U.S. NATIONALS OUTSIDE THE UNITED STATES; CONSPIRACY TO MURDER U.S. NATIONALS OUTSIDE THE UNITED STATES; ATTACK ON A FEDERAL FACILITY RESULTING IN DEATH

WANTED BY THE FBI

ALIASES: Abu Hafs, Abu Hafs El-Masry El-Khabir, Taysir, Sheikh Taysir Abdullah, Abu Khadijah

DESCRIPTION

DATE OF BIRTH: Unknown	**SCARS AND MARKS:** None known
PLACE OF BIRTH: Egypt	**HAIR:** Dark brown/black
HEIGHT: 6'4" to 6'6"	**EYES:** Brown
WEIGHT: Unknown	**COMPLEXION:** Olive
BUILD: Thin	**SEX:** Male
LANGUAGES: Arabic	**CITIZENSHIP:** Egyptian

REMARKS: Atef is alleged to be Usama Bin Laden's second in command of the terrorist organization, Al-Qaeda.

CAUTION

Muhammad Atef has been indicted for his alleged involvement with the August 7, 1998, bombings of the United States Embassies in Dar es Salaam, Tanzania, and Nairobi, Kenya. The Rewards For Justice Program, United States Department of State, is offering a reward of up to $25 million for information leading directly to the apprehension or conviction of Muhammad Atef.

WANTED
TERRORISM

ALI SAED BIN ALI EL-HOORIE
$25,000,000 REWARD

CONSPIRACY TO KILL U.S. NATIONALS; CONSPIRACY TO MURDER U.S. EMPLOYEES; CONSPIRACY TO USE WEAPONS OF MASS DESTRUCTION AGAINST U.S. NATIONALS; CONSPIRACY TO DESTROY PROPERTY OF THE U. S.; CONSPIRACY TO ATTACK NATIONAL DEFENSE UTILITIES; BOMBING RESULTING IN DEATH; USE OF WEAPONS OF MASS DESTRUCTION AGAINST U.S. NATIONALS; MURDER WHILE USING DESTRUCTIVE DEVICE DURING A CRIME OF VIOLENCE; MURDER OF FEDERAL EMPLOYEES; ATTEMPTED MURDER OF FEDERAL EMPLOYEES

WANTED BY THE FBI

ALIASES: Ali Saed Bin Ali Al-Houri

DESCRIPTION

DATES OF BIRTH USED: July 10, 1965; July 11, 1965	**SCARS AND MARKS:** El-Hoorie has a mole on his face.
PLACE OF BIRTH: El Dibabiya, Saudi Arabia	
HEIGHT: 5'2"	**HAIR:** Black
WEIGHT: 130 pounds	**EYES:** Black
BUILD: Unknown	**COMPLEXION:** Olive
LANGUAGES: Arabic	**SEX:** Male
	CITIZENSHIP: Saudi Arabian

CAUTION

Ali Saed Bin El-Hoorie has been indicted in the Eastern District of Virginia for the June 25, 1996, bombing of the Khobar Towers military housing complex in Dhahran, Kingdom of Saudi Arabia. The Rewards For Justice Program, United States Department of State, is offering a reward of up to $25 million for information leading directly to the apprehension or indictment of Ali Saed Bin Ali El-Hoorie.

WANTED
TERRORISM

SAIF AL-ADEL
$25,000,000 REWARD

CONSPIRACY TO KILL U.S. NATIONALS, TO MURDER, TO DESTROY BUILDINGS
AND PROPERTY OF THE UNITED STATES, AND TO DESTROY THE NATIONAL
DEFENSE UTILITIES OF THE UNITED STATES

WANTED BY THE FBI

ALIASES: Muhamad Ibrahim Makkawi, Seif Al Adel, Ibrahim Al-Madani

DESCRIPTION

DATES OF BIRTH USED:	April 11, 1963; April 11, 1960	SCARS AND MARKS:	None known
PLACE OF BIRTH:	Egypt	HAIR:	Dark
HEIGHT:	Unknown	EYES:	Dark
WEIGHT:	Unknown	COMPLEXION:	Olive
BUILD:	Unknown	SEX:	Male
LANGUAGES:	Arabic	CITIZENSHIP:	Egyptian

REMARKS: Al-Adel is thought to be affiliated with the Egyptian Islamic Jihad (EIJ), and is believed to be a high-ranking member of the Al-Qaeda organization, currently in Afghanistan.

CAUTION

Saif Al-Adel is wanted in connection with the August 7, 1998, bombings of the United States Embassies in Dar es Salaam, Tanzania, and Nairobi, Kenya. The Rewards For Justice Program, United States Department of State, is offering a reward of up to $25 million for information leading directly to the apprehension or conviction of Saif Al-Adel.

WANTED
TERRORISM

IBRAHIM SALIH MOHAMMED AL-YACOUB
$25,000,000 REWARD

CONSPIRACY TO KILL U.S. NATIONALS; CONSPIRACY TO MURDER U.S. EMPLOYEES;
CONSPIRACY TO USE WEAPONS OF MASS DESTRUCTION AGAINST U.S. NATIONALS;
CONSPIRACY TO DESTROY PROPERTY OF THE U. S.; CONSPIRACY TO ATTACK
NATIONAL DEFENSE UTILITIES; BOMBING RESULTING IN DEATH; USE OF WEAPONS OF
MASS DESTRUCTION AGAINST U.S. NATIONALS; MURDER WHILE USING DESTRUCTIVE
DEVICE DURING A CRIME OF VIOLENCE; MURDER OF FEDERAL EMPLOYEES;
ATTEMPTED MURDER OF FEDERAL EMPLOYEES

WANTED BY THE FBI

ALIASES: None known

DESCRIPTION

DATE OF BIRTH: October 16, 1966	SCARS AND MARKS: None known
PLACE OF BIRTH: Tarut, Saudi Arabia	HAIR: Black
HEIGHT: 5'4"	EYES: Brown
WEIGHT: 150 pounds	COMPLEXION: Olive
BUILD: Unknown	SEX: Male
LANGUAGES: Arabic	CITIZENSHIP: Saudi Arabian

CAUTION

Ibrahim Salih Mohammed Al-Yacoub has been indicted in the Eastern District of Virginia for the June 25, 1996, bombing of the Khobar Towers military housing complex in Dhahran, Kingdom of Saudi Arabia. The Rewards For Justice Program, United States Department of State, is offering a reward of up to $25 million for information leading directly to the apprehension or indictment of Ibrahim Salih Mohammed Al-Yacoub.

WANTED

Diplomatic Security Service
U.S. Department of State

KIDNAPPING & MURDER of DANIEL PEARL

$5,000,000 REWARD

INFORMATION IS WANTED BY THE DIPLOMATIC SECURITY SERVICE U.S. DEPARTMENT OF STATE

DANIEL PEARL   1963 – 2002

The Rewards for Justice program is offering up to 5 million dollars for information leading to the arrest or conviction in any country of those responsible for the kidnapping and murder of Daniel Pearl.

The Department of State confirmed his death on 21 February 2002 in the following statement.

Statement by Richard Boucher, Spokesman

"Our Embassy in Pakistan has confirmed today that they have received evidence that Wall Street Journal reporter Daniel Pearl is dead. We have informed Mr. Pearl's family and expressed our sincere condolences.

The murder of Mr. Pearl is an outrage and we condemn it. Both the United States and Pakistan are committed to identifying all the perpetrators of this crime and bringing them to justice. We will continue to work closely with Pakistani authorities, who have made every effort to locate and free Mr. Pearl."

Persons wishing to report information about the murderers of Daniel Pearl, the groups involved or other terrorist attacks or the planning of future terrorist attacks against U.S. persons or property should contact the authorities or the nearest U.S. embassy or consulate. In the United States, call your local office of the Federal Bureau of Investigation or the Bureau of Diplomatic Security at 1-800-USREWARDS, or write to:

Rewards for Justice
P.O. Box 96781
Washington, D.C. 20522-0303, USA

Internet: mail@rewardsforjustice.net
Voice: 1-800-USREWARDS

WANTED FOR

MURDER

DRUG DISTRIBUTION

SEXUAL ASSAULT

FRAUD

BANK ROBBERY

KIDNAPPING

WANTED
FOR MURDER

MICHAEL ALFONSO
$10,000 REWARD

Unlawful flight to avoid prosecution – murder

WANTED BY THE FBI

Photographs taken in 2000   Photograph taken in 1997   1994 Pontiac Firebird
Illinois License Plates D294256

ALIASES: Michael Johnsen, Milton Lenon

DESCRIPTION

DATE OF BIRTH: June 26, 1969	**SCARS, MARKS, TATTOOS:** Alfonso has a scar on his chest.
PLACE OF BIRTH: Illinois	
HEIGHT: 5'5"	**OCCUPATION:** Chef
WEIGHT: 150 lbs	**SEX:** Male
HAIR: Black	**RACE:** Black
EYES: Brown	**NATIONALITY:** American

REMARKS: Alfonso is a registered sex offender in Illinois. He is fluent in Spanish and has a muscular build. He may be driving a black 1994 Pontiac Firebird with Illinois license plates reading D294256. Alfonso was born Michael Johnsen but changed his name to Michael Alfonso.

CAUTION

On the morning of June 6, 2001, a woman was shot to death in the parking lot of a fast food restaurant in Wheaton, Illinois, where she worked. Following an investigation by the Wheaton Police Department, Michael Alfonso, the victim's former boyfriend, was named as a suspect in the murder. On June 6, 2001, a state arrest warrant was issued by the Circuit Court of DuPage County, Illinois, charging Alfonso with first degree murder and aggravated stalking. Then, on June 7, 2001, a federal warrant was issued by the U.S. District Court, Chicago, Illinois, charging Alfonso with unlawful flight to avoid prosecution.

SHOULD BE CONSIDERED ARMED AND DANGEROUS

WANTED

ATTEMPTED MURDER

STEPHEN HOWARD ANDERSON

$20,000 REWARD

WANTED BY BUREAU OF ALCOHOL, TOBACCO AND FIREARMS

DESCRIPTION

DATE OF BIRTH: July 16, 1947 **EYES:** Green
HEIGHT: 6'2" **SEX:** Male
WEIGHT: 235 lbs **RACE:** White
HAIR: Dark/Short

CAUTION

On October 15, 2001 Stephen Anderson, a member of the Kentucky Militia attempted to kill a sheriffs Deputy by shooting at his police cruiser with an assault rifle. Deputy Sheriff Scott Elder stopped Anderson's pick up truck to advise him that he had a broken taillight. Anderson then opened fire on the Deputy with what was believed to be an AK-47, hitting the vehicle 25 times.

Elder pursued Anderson, but after a few minutes, Anderson turned around and began shooting at the Deputy again. Neither Elder, or his girl friend that was in the car was seriously injured, but she did get cut from a piece of flying glass from the shattered windshield.

Anderson's wrecked pickup truck was found the next day. According to the police, it contained pipe bombs, and a large amount of ammunition.

A spokesman for the Kentucky State Militia said Anderson had been kicked out of the organization because he broadcast an amateur radio show on his illegal three-hour show that frequently voiced anti-Jewish sentiments.

He is still at large, and considered to be armed and extremely dangerous. The Kentucky State Police, and the Bureau of Alcohol, Tobacco and Firearms are offering a $20,000 reward for information leading to his arrest.

WANTED
FOR MURDER

RONALD JEFFREY BAX
REWARD

WANTED BY THE ROYAL CANADIAN MOUNTED POLICE

DESCRIPTION

DATE OF BIRTH:	November 25, 1961	**HAIR:**	Blonde
HEIGHT:	5'7"	**EYES:**	Blue
WEIGHT:	150 lbs	**SEX:**	Male
SCARS, MARKS, TATTOOS:	Winged horse on upper right arm	**RACE:**	White
		NATIONALITY:	Canadian
		RCMP FILE:	92GE08697

CAUTION

Around the town of Carcross, Yukon Territory, Ronald Bax was known as a sculptor, taxidermist, outdoorsman and an expert with guns. Now he's known as a suspected killer. After a long history of marital discord and allegations of spousal abuse, Ronald's wife, Lynn, sought refuge in a shelter for battered women on March 1, 1992. Her only visitor that night was her best friend, Krystal Senyk. Theirs was a close friendship that sources say Bax deeply resented. When Krystal returned to her home at around 11 p.m. someone was lying in wait for her. A single shot from close range left Krystal dead in the doorway of her own home. Ronald Bax vanished immediately and is the only known suspect in the murder. Bax has family in Michigan and there is a strong possibility that he is hiding somewhere in the U.S.

SHOULD BE CONSIDERED ARMED AND DANGEROUS

WANTED
FOR MURDER

BOUNSOUAY CHANTHAVONG

REWARD

Unlawful flight to avoid prosecution – murder

WANTED BY THE FBI

ALIASES: Bounsouay Tony Chanthavong, Hum Chanthavong, Tony Hum, "Hum"

DESCRIPTION

DATE OF BIRTH: May 5, 1975	**SCARS, MARKS, TATTOOS:** Chanthavong has a tattoo of a Buddha on his back and unknown tattoos on both of his arms.
PLACE OF BIRTH: Thailand	
HEIGHT: 5'7"	
WEIGHT: 135 lbs	**RACE:** Asian
HAIR: Black	**NATIONALITY:** Thai
EYES: Brown	**OCCUPATION:** Unknown
SEX: Male	**NCIC:** W090503000

REMARKS: Chanthavong has ties to Nashville, Tennessee and may currently be in California.

CAUTION

Bounsouay Chanthavong is wanted for his alleged involvement in the murder of a man in Nashville, Tennessee. On August 29, 1999, Chanthavong allegedly went to the residence of the victim in order to settle an ongoing domestic dispute and became involved in an argument. After Chanthavong allegedly punched the victim's wife in the mouth, the victim came out of another room to confront Chanthavong, at which time Chanthavong allegedly shot him. On August 31, 1999, Chanthavong was charged in Davidson County, Tennessee, with criminal homicide. A federal arrest warrant was subsequently issued for Chanthavong charging him with unlawful flight to avoid prosecution.

SHOULD BE CONSIDERED ARMED AND DANGEROUS

WANTED

FOR MURDER

MARCUS CURRY
$16,000 REWARD

WANTED BY SAN DIEGO SHERIFF

DESCRIPTION

DATE OF BIRTH: November 2, 1975	HAIR:	Black
HEIGHT: 6'0"	EYES:	Brown
WEIGHT: 200 lbs	SEX:	Male
	RACE:	Black

THE DETAILS SURROUNDING THE CRIME

The San Diego Sheriff's homicide investigators are looking for the following suspect who was involved in a homicide (San Diego Sheriff's Department case #99033819H). Marcus Curry is to be considered armed and Dangerous. Marcus Curry has a no bail felony arrest warrant in the N.C.I.C. computer system. Suspect is a Rollin' 60's Crip gang member from the South Central Los Angeles area. If you have information about this murder or his whereabouts, please contact detectives Rick Empson or William Donahue 24 hours a day at (619) 565-5200, or call the WeTip Hotline at (800) 78-CRIME.

WANTED
FOR MURDER

ADRIAN DELGADO-VASQUEZ

REWARD

Unlawful flight to avoid prosecution – second degree murder

WANTED BY THE FBI

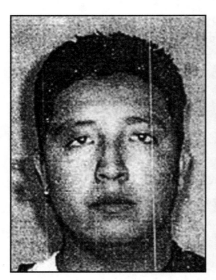 

DESCRIPTION

DATE OF BIRTH USED: December 20, 1981	**RACE:** White (Hispanic)
PLACE OF BIRTH: Tlapatzingo, Oaxaco, Mexico	**SCARS, MARKS:** Delgado-Vasquez has a tattoo of
HEIGHT: 5'7"	the word "SURENO" on the left side of his chest.
WEIGHT: 160 lbs	**OCCUPATION:** Unknown
HAIR: Black	**NATIONALITY:** Mexican
EYES: Brown	**NCIC #:** W731735048
SEX: Male	

REMARKS: Delgado-Vasquez has ties to Washington State and California, and may currently be travelling in Mexico.

CAUTION

Adrian Delgado-Vasquez is wanted for his alleged involvement in the murder of a man. On April 18, 2001, Delgado-Vasquez stabbed a man in the back while on the Tulalip Indian Reservation near Marysville, Washington. The two men were allegedly arguing over a female with whom they were both romantically involved. The man later died of his wounds. Delgado-Vasquez was subsequently charged with second degree murder in Snohomish County, Washington. A federal arrest warrant was issued on June 29, 2001, charging Delgado-Vasquez with unlawful flight to avoid prosecution in the United States District Court for the Western District of Washington.

WANTED
FOR MURDER

RANDOLPH FRANKLIN DIAL
$25,000 REWARD
Unlawful flight to avoid prosecution – murder
WANTED BY THE FBI

ALIASES: Randolph Franklin Johnston, Randolph Franklin, Randy F. Johnston, Randolph Franklin Johnson, Randy F. Johnson, Frank Johnson, Frank Randolph, "Doc", "Doc" Franklin, "Doc" Johnson

DESCRIPTION

DATE OF BIRTH: September 26, 1944
PLACE OF BIRTH: Oklahoma
HEIGHT: 5'9"
WEIGHT: 170 lbs
HAIR: Gray
EYES: Brown
OCCUPATION: Artist

SCARS, MARKS, TATTOOS: Dial has a scar on his chin, back, chest, and left calf.
SEX: Male
RACE: White
NATIONALITY: American
NCIC: W823113627

REMARKS: Dial has taught art at a university in Mexico and has worked commercially as an artist. He still has strong ties to various areas in Mexico. He is fluent in Spanish and is very familiar with the Mexican culture. Dial may also travel to southwestern areas of the United States. He has an interest in southwestern art. Dial suffers from a heart condition which may require prescription medication. His teeth are in poor condition and he may be missing one or two lower front teeth.

CAUTION

In August of 1994, Randolph Franklin Dial escaped from the Oklahoma State Reformatory in Granite, Oklahoma, while serving a life sentence for murder. Bobbi Louaine Parker, the wife of the assistant warden of the prison at that time, has been missing since Dial's escape. A few days after the escape, Parker's minivan was found abandoned in Wichita Falls, Texas. While incarcerated, Dial initiated and expanded an art program at the prison which allowed inmates to make art pieces, including paintings, sculptures, and pottery. This program involved Parker and the use of her garage, which was on the prison grounds, as one of the areas where the art work was done. This enabled Dial to befriend Parker.

SHOULD BE CONSIDERED ARMED AND DANGEROUS

WANTED
FOR ATTEMPTED MURDER

CHI Q. DU

REWARD

Unlawful flight to avoid prosecution – attempted murder

WANTED BY THE FBI

ALIASES: Du Chi, Chi Du Q

DESCRIPTION

DATE OF BIRTH USED: April 4, 1970	HAIR: Black
PLACE OF BIRTH: Vietnam	EYES: Black
HEIGHT: 5'6"	SEX: Male
WEIGHT: 125 lbs	RACE: Asian
SCARS, MARKS, TATTOOS: Du has a scar on the right side of his face that runs from his hairline to his eyebrow.	NATIONALITY: Vietnamese
	OCCUPATION: Unknown
	NCIC: W037254721

REMARKS: Du is often mistaken for being Hispanic. He slouches when he walks and has bad teeth.

CAUTION

On October 28, 1997, Chi Q. Du allegedly stabbed his former girlfriend and an acquaintance on the campus of a university in Fairborn, Ohio. Du allegedly waited outside the university library and then stabbed the victims multiple times. A state arrest warrant was issued by the State of Ohio on October 29, 1997, charging Du with attempted murder. On November 6, 1997, a federal arrest warrant was issued by the Southern District of Ohio, charging Du with unlawful flight to avoid prosecution.

SHOULD BE CONSIDERED ARMED AND DANGEROUS

WANTED
FOR MURDER

LEONARD RAY HARPER, JR.
REWARD

Unlawful flight to avoid prosecution – murder

WANTED BY THE FBI

Photograph taken in 1991

ALIASES: Ray Harper, Hap Harper

DESCRIPTION

DATE OF BIRTH: October 4, 1970
PLACE OF BIRTH: Dallas, Texas
HEIGHT: 5'9"
WEIGHT: 160 lbs
OCCUPATION: Harper sold golf equipment, often working at trade fairs.
HAIR: Brown

EYES: Green
SCARS, MARKS, TATTOOS: Harper has a scar on his right cheek
SEX: Male
RACE: White
NATIONALITY: American
NCIC: W158114320

REMARKS: Harper is reported to be a heavy drug user who likes the partying scene, fast cars, and frequents gentlemen's clubs. He is an avid SCUBA diver and may be working as an instructor. Harper may have traveled to Spain or other parts of Europe.

CAUTION

On July 19, 1997, an argument broke out between a man and a woman while they were driving in San Antonio, Texas. During the argument, the man struck the woman, who was pregnant at the time. The woman's husband, Leonard Ray Harper, Jr., swore revenge on the man, who had been one of his associates. On August 24, 1997, Harper allegedly coaxed the man into going partying with him under the pretense that he wanted to make amends and renew their friendship. After allegedly luring the man into his car, Harper drove the man to a remote spot and killed him. Soon after the murder, Harper left Texas with his wife and child and drove cross country, staying in different cities for a week or two at a time. During this time, he is alleged to have been using drugs and then started exhibiting violent mood swings. Police were eventually alerted and Harper was arrested for murder. Harper posted bond on May 13, 1998 and failed to appear in court on December 4, 1998. A federal arrest warrant was issued on May 13, 1999, in the Western District of Texas, San Antonio, Texas charging Harper with unlawful flight to avoid prosecution.

SHOULD BE CONSIDERED ARMED AND DANGEROUS

WANTED
FOR MURDER

JOHN MILTON FEIGA
$10,000 REWARD
Unlawful flight to avoid prosecution – murder
WANTED BY THE FBI

ALIAS: John Milton Feiga

DESCRIPTION

DATE OF BIRTH USED: December 14, 1960	**SCARS, MARKS:** Feiga has the following tattoos: the word "Feiga" on the back of his left hand, his right calf, and his right bicep; "John" on his left leg, and the letters "JF" on his left forearm and right bicep.
PLACE OF BIRTH: Louisiana	
HEIGHT: 5'10"	
WEIGHT: 183 lbs	
HAIR: Black	
EYES: Brown	**OCCUPATIONS:** Electric company technician, truck driver, bus driver
SEX: Male	
RACE: Black	**NATIONALITY:** American
	NCIC #: W046064716

REMARKS: Feiga has a pierced left ear. Feiga may travel to New Roads and Baton Rouge, Louisiana; Mobile, Alabama, and Texas.

CAUTION

John Feiga is wanted for allegedly murdering his estranged girlfriend in Valrico, Florida, a suburb of Tampa. Feiga was reportedly angered after the victim ended their relationship. The 33-year-old victim's body, with multiple stab wounds, was discovered in her apartment on December 8, 1997. The victim was last seen alive on the morning of December 7, 1997. Feiga was reportedly last seen on that same day driving the victim's vehicle, which later was found by law enforcement authorities in a hospital parking lot in Lafayette, Louisiana.

CRIME ALERT
JOHN MILTON FEIGA

In early December 1997, Erica Richardson was murdered at her home in Valrico, FL. Two years earlier, she and John Milton Feiga became acquainted and began to date. After a while, Mr. Feiga moved into Ms. Richardsons new home in the outskirts of Tampa. He has been described as a smooth talking ladies man, who was constantly bringing Erica gifts, and sending her love notes.

Unfortunately, Feiga soon became overly possessive and violent, so much so that he was twice arrested for battery, causing Erica to file a restraining order against him. On December 8th Ericas mother, Imogene Richardson tried to call her 33-year-old daughter who was employed as the manger of the Valrico Wal-Mart Pharmacy. Erica had not come to work that day, nor had she called in sick.

Naturally, being concerned, Mrs. Richardson went to her daughters home. The doors were locked and most of the blinds and curtains were closed. No one answered the door, but when she managed to look through the kitchen window, she saw a knife and a lot of blood. When Detectives entered the house and discovered the body, they determined that Erica had been stabbed 62 times.

Feiga was missing, and so was Ericas car, a Honda. Two weeks after the murder, the Honda was found in a hospital parking lot in Lafayette, Louisiana, It is important to note that Feiga was raised in and still has family in a nearby small town called New Roads.

Ericas parents continue to mourn for their daughter and schedule candlelight vigils as a memorial to her. They have also raised a reward of $10,000 for Feigas arrest. Although he is wanted only for grand theft Auto, Detectives are anxious to question him about Erica Richardsons murder.

Victim Erica Richardson

WANTED
MURDER

HAZEL LEOTA HEAD
$5,000 REWARD

Unlawful flight to avoid prosecution – first degree murder; arson; failure to appear

WANTED BY THE FBI

Photograph taken in 1991

ALIASES: Hazel Morgan, Hazel L. Morgan, Willow Shield, Willow L. Shields, Willow Shield, Hazel Woodman, Hazel Leota Woodman, Hazel Foley, Hazel Leota Foley, Kelly Morgan, Hazel Spurbeck, Willow Spurbeck, Hazel Haynes, Hazel Leota Haynes, Hazel Vincent, Deianna Ray, Hazel Fatuch, Hazel Leota Fatuch, Treasa Tess Jean Coyle, Treasa Tess Venable, Tess Venable, Tess Coyle, Treasa Venable, Treasa Coyle, Hazel Leota Sperbeck, Willow Sperbeck, Deianna Wray

DESCRIPTION

DATE OF BIRTH USED: December 19. 1949	**SCARS AND MARKS:** Has a scar near her right eye.
PLACE OF BIRTH: Dayton, Ohio	**HAIR:** Blonde (reddish)
HEIGHT: 5'2"	**EYES:** Green/Hazel
WEIGHT: 120 pounds	**SEX:** Female
OCCUPATION: Waitress	**RACE:** White
	NATIONALITY: American

REMARKS: Head has a gap between her front teeth. She may have gained weight. Head often works as a waitress, hangs out at truck stops, and likes to travel with truck drivers. She is a smoker, likes to drink vodka, and frequent casinos. She has been married several times, possibly to as many as 10 men, and is known to place personal ads seeking men. Head has a history of moving and living throughout the United States, and may have ties to Wheat Ridge, Colorado.

CAUTION
Hazel Leota Head is wanted for the murder of a man in Benton, Louisiana, in 1998. The victim was shot in the back of the head while he sat in his trailer. In September of 1998, a state arrest warrant was issued by the 26th Judicial District Court, Bossier Parish, Louisiana, charging Head with murder. A federal arrest warrant was subsequently issued in the Western District of Louisiana in January of 1999, charging Head with unlawful flight to avoid prosecution. In addition, Head has been wanted since 1991 by local law enforcement authorities in Nebraska where she is charged with arson and failure to appear. She is accused there of burning down a boyfriend's trailer.

WANTED
BURGLARY, MURDER

FETHI JELASSI

Unlawful flight to avoid prosecution – aggravated murder, aggravated burglary

WANTED BY THE FBI

ALIASES: Frank Jelassi, Frank Adams, Phillip Adams, Phillip Jelassi, Omar B. Messadud, Omar Messaoud, Fethi Messaoud, "Bashir"

DESCRIPTION

DATE OF BIRTH: July 22, 1954
PLACE OF BIRTH: Tunisia
HEIGHT: 5'7"
WEIGHT: 185 lbs
HAIR: Black
EYES: Brown

SCARS, MARKS, TATTOOS: Jelassi may have a tattoo of a female on his upper left arm.
SEX: Male
RACE: White (North African)
NCIC: W351055513

CAUTION

Fethi Jelassi is wanted for the shooting deaths of a man and his mother in Cleveland, Ohio. On June 22, 2000, Jelassi allegedly shot David Settle more than ten times over a disputed relationship. Settle's mother was shot numerous times in the head as well. On September 27, 2000, a state arrest warrant was issued by the State of Ohio, Cuyahoga County Court of Common Pleas, charging Jelassi with two counts of aggravated murder and one count of aggravated burglary. On September 29, 2000, a federal arrest warrant was issued for unlawful flight to avoid prosecution by the United States Magistrate, Northern District of Ohio, Cleveland, Ohio.

SHOULD BE CONSIDERED ARMED AND DANGEROUS

WANTED
FOR MURDER

CECIL C. JONES

REWARD

Unlawful flight to avoid prosecution – murder

WANTED BY THE FBI

Photograph taken in 1997

ALIASES: Cecil Jones, Cecil Cleo Jones, Cleo Jones

DESCRIPTION

DATES OF BIRTH USED: September 14, 1969, September 14, 1968
PLACE OF BIRTH: Louisiana
HEIGHT: 5'9"
WEIGHT: 190 lbs
HAIR: Bald
EYES: Brown
SEX: Male

RACE: Black
SCARS, MARKS: Jones has unknown tattoos on his chest and left arm. He also has tattoos of a heart, knife, rose and wings on his right arm.
OCCUPATION: Unknown
NATIONALITY: American
NCIC #: W136027198

REMARKS: Jones is bald. He may be residing in the Los Angeles, California area where he has relatives and friends. He may be driving a late-model, green BMW automobile.

CAUTION

Cecil C. Jones is wanted for the murder of a Louisiana man on January 9, 1999. Jones allegedly shot and killed the victim following a personal dispute at a night club in Monroe, Louisiana. On January 12, 1999, a state arrest warrant was issued in the 4th Judicial District, State of Louisiana, charging Jones with second degree murder. Jones is believed to have fled Louisiana shortly after the murder. A federal arrest warrant was subsequently issued by the U.S. District Court for the Western District of Louisiana charging Jones with unlawful flight to avoid prosecution.

WANTED

FOR MURDER

DAVID GIBSON LINDSAY

Unlawful flight to avoid prosecution – first degree murder, theft of a motor vehicle over $300

WANTED BY THE FBI

ALIASES: James Wolf, Steve Walden

DESCRIPTION

DATE OF BIRTH: February 18, 1950	**SCARS, MARKS, TATTOOS:** Lindsay has a scar on his abdomen.
PLACE OF BIRTH: Illinois	
HEIGHT: 5'8"	**SEX:** Male
WEIGHT: 150 lbs	**RACE:** White
OCCUPATION: Boat dock worker.	**NATIONALITY:** American
HAIR: Gray	**NCIC:** W672275779
EYES: Brown	

REMARKS: Lindsay is homeless. He has been described as having shoulder length hair, a beard, and a bad rash all over his body. Lindsay may be driving the victim's red, 4-door, 1996 Ford Crown Victoria, with Illinois license plates Y263291.

CAUTION

On December 18, 2001, Illinois law enforcement authorities discovered the body of a man in his Decatur, Illinois apartment. They also discovered that his car, a red Ford Crown Victoria, was missing. During the course of the investigation, the victim's vehicle was located at a resort in Daytona Beach, Florida, after the local police there had received complaints from tenants that a man was living in the vehicle in the resort's parking lot. When police arrived, the man was not in the vehicle. After Florida law enforcement authorities were advised of the murder and returned to the resort's parking lot, the car was gone. Further investigation led police to believe that the man in the car was David Gibson Lindsay, a homeless man who had been an acquaintance of the victim. On January 7, 2002, a state arrest warrant was issued by the Circuit Court of the Sixth Judicial Circuit, Macon County, Illinois, charging David Gibson Lindsay with first degree murder and theft of a motor vehicle over $300. On January 10, 2002, a federal arrest warrant was issued in the Central District of Illinois, Urbana, Illinois, charging Lindsay with unlawful flight to avoid prosecution.

WANTED
FOR MURDER

DESIREE DAWN LINGO-PERKINS
REWARD

Unlawful flight to avoid prosecution – capitol murder

WANTED BY THE FBI

| Photograph taken in 1999 | Photograph taken in 1999 | Photograph altered in 2001 | Additional photograph |

ALIASES: Esperanza Perkins, Espiranza Perkins, Perkins Lingo, Esperanza Lingo, Esperanza Lingo-Perkins, Lingo Perkins

DESCRIPTION

DATE OF BIRTH: January 11, 1969
PLACE OF BIRTH: Texas
HEIGHT: 5'6"
WEIGHT: 170 to 200 pounds
NCIC: W950571168
OCCUPATIONS: Unknown
SEX: Female

SCARS AND MARKS: Desiree Lingo-Perkins has a scar on her abdomen and a tattoo of a butterfly on her right calf with the names "Teanna", Sean", and Rachel written beneath it.
HAIR: Blonde
EYES: Green
NATIONALITY: American

REMARKS: Desiree Lingo-Perkins has ties to Beaumont, Texas; Connecticut and the Texas/Mexican border. She has become familiar with the Mexican immigrant community in Texas, and as a result, she is believed to be traveling throughout southern Texas. She may travel with truck drivers. She is known to be involved in prostitution.

Lingo-Perkins has tested positive for Hepatitis C. She also suffers from a bipolar disorder and has taken the following medications: Trazadone, Lithium, and Prozac.

CAUTION

Desiree Dawn Lingo-Perkins is wanted for her alleged involvement in the kidnapping and murder of a Texas man. On March 10, 2000, the victim was kidnapped in Troup, Texas. A ransom note was received a short time later by his family. The next day, the victim's body was discovered in rural Cherokee County, Texas. Three males have since been arrested on state warrants charging them with capital murder in connection with this case. Lingo-Perkins, an alleged active participant in the planning and execution of the crime, has also been charged in a state warrant for capital murder and a federal warrant for unlawful flight to avoid prosecution.

WANTED
FOR MURDER

GLENDON JACKSON LITTLE

Unlawful flight to avoid prosecution – murder, assault and
battery with a deadly weapon with intent to kill

WANTED BY THE FBI

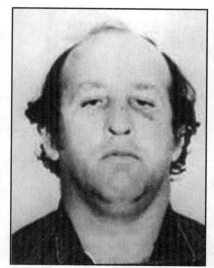
Photo taken 1978

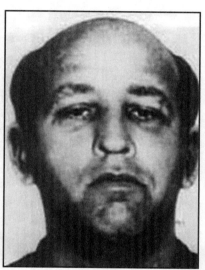
Age enhanced photo

ALIAS: Jack Little

DESCRIPTION

DATE OF BIRTH: September 8, 1941	**SCARS, MARKS:** Scar on left eyelid
PLACE OF BIRTH: Arkansas	**SEX:** Male
HEIGHT: 6'0"	**RACE:** White
WEIGHT: 200 lbs	**OCCUPATION:** Electrician
HAIR: Brown/Gray (bald spot on top)	**NATIONALITY:** American
EYES: Brown	**NCIC #:** W327877070

REMARKS: Little is a former U.S. military marksman. He is an avid hunter and gun collector. It is believed that Little has ties to Tennessee. Little has an old back injury and may walk with a limp.

CAUTION

On January 5, 1984, it is alleged that Glendon Jackson Little went to the Oklahoma residence of his ex-wife and shot her along with her boyfriend. Little allegedly shot the boyfriend three times, striking him in his chest, his right cheek, and his right temple. He died from his injuries. Afterwards, Little allegedly shot his ex-wife in the face, but she survived the attack.

On January 9, 1984, Little was charged locally in Oklahoma County with murder and assault and battery with a deadly weapon with intent to kill. A federal arrest warrant was issued by the United States District Court, Western District of Oklahoma on January 25, 1984 charging Little with unlawful flight to avoid prosecution.

WANTED

FOR MURDER

RAMIRO LOPEZ & ABEL REYES

murder, unlawful flight to avoid prosecution

WANTED BY THE FBI

Ramiro Lopez

Abel Reyes

DESCRIPTION

RAMIRO LOPEZ is a Hispanic male born in Oaxaca, Mexico, on May 13, 1967. He is five feet, three inches tall and weighs 160 pounds. He has black hair and brown eyes. Lopez has a California driver's license and travels between the U.S. and Mexico. He has used the aliases Ramiro Luengas, Ramiro Garcia, Raul Gomez, Raul Losano.

ABEL REYES is a Hispanic male born on October 16, 1973, in Oaxaca, Mexico. He is five feet, five inches tall and weighs 160 pounds. He has black hair and brown eyes. Reyes has used the aliases Margarito Gonzales and Margarito Lugos. He has a California driver's license and may be traveling with Lopez, between the U.S. and Mexico. Both men should be considered armed and dangerous.

DETAILS

Abel Reyes and Ramiro Lopez are wanted for beating and stabbing to death a New Brunswick, New Jersey, man, Drumax Cruz, on September 4, 1993. The two men fled to Bethlehem, Pennsylvania, and then to their hometown, Oaxaca, Mexico. New Jersey authorities have charged them with murder. A federal warrant charges them with unlawful flight to avoid prosecution.

WANTED
FOR MURDER

JUAN CARLOS MARTINEZ
REWARD
Unlawful flight to avoid prosecution – murder
WANTED BY THE FBI

ALIAS: Juan D. Martinez

DESCRIPTION

DATES OF BIRTH USED: December 2, 1978, December 14, 1981	**SEX:** Male
PLACE OF BIRTH: Mexico	**RACE:** White (Hispanic)
HEIGHT: 5'6"	**SCARS, MARKS:** None known
WEIGHT: 135 lbs	**OCCUPATIONS:** Welder, machinist, metal fabricator, interpreter (Spanish/English)
HAIR: Black	**NATIONALITY:** American
EYES: Brown	**NCIC #:** W165633135

REMARKS: Martinez speaks fluent English and Spanish. He has ties to Alabama, Texas, Florida, North Carolina, Minnesota, and Mexico.

CAUTION

Juan Carlos Martinez is wanted for his alleged involvement in the murder of a man in the Albertville, Alabama area. On June 2, 1999, Martinez allegedly shot the victim several times with a handgun in the parking lot of an industrial company where they were employed. The murder reportedly resulted from an ongoing personal dispute. On June 3, 1999, a state arrest warrant was issued by the District Court of Marshall County, Alabama charging Martinez with murder. He was subsequently charged in a federal arrest warrant with unlawful flight to avoid prosecution. Martinez is believed to have fled from Albertville in a vehicle which was later found abandoned near Interstate 59 and Rainsville, Alabama. Martinez may have fled to Mexico, but is believed to maintain contact with individuals currently in the United States.

WANTED
FOR MURDER

MARVIN ACLARO MERCADO
$20,000 REWARD

Unlawful flight to avoid prosecution – murder, attempted murder, burglary, conspiracy to commit murder with a firearm

WANTED BY THE FBI

ALIASES: Marvin Mercado, Marvin A. Mercado, Marvin Claro Mercado, "Slim", "Boo Boo"

DESCRIPTION

DATES OF BIRTH USED: July 16, 1973, July 1, 1973
PLACE OF BIRTH: Panorama, California
HEIGHT: 6'0"
WEIGHT: 160 lbs
OCCUPATION: Unknown
HAIR: Black
EYES: Brown

SCARS, MARKS, TATTOOS: Mercado has a tattoo of a dragon on his back.
SEX: Male
RACE: Asian
NATIONALITY: American (Philippine descent)
NCIC: W978841947

REMARKS: Marvin Mercado is known to travel to the Philippine Islands.

CAUTION

Marvin Aclaro Mercado is wanted for his alleged involvement in a series of murders and attempted murders which occurred in 1995 in the Los Angeles, California area. Mercado is a leader of an Asian street gang, known as the "Asian Boyz", whose members are thought to be responsible for the murders. The victims were rival gang members and others not associated with any gangs. The "Asian Boyz" are also believed to have committed other crimes which include home invasion robberies, burglaries, extortions, and arson. In 1997, several "Asian Boyz" gang members were indicted by a State Grand Jury. Then, in 1999, after a four-month trial, the "Asian Boyz" gang members involved in the trial were convicted and received life sentences. However, Mercado is believed to have fled to the Philippines with his brother, Pierre Mercado, who is also an "Asian Boyz" gang member. Pierre Mercado is a federal fugitive wanted for the underlying state charge of attempted murder.

SHOULD BE CONSIDERED ARMED AND DANGEROUS

WANTED

FOR CAPITAL MURDER

PAUL ALLEN MOSES

Unlawful flight to avoid prosecution – capital murder

WANTED BY THE FBI

Photograph taken in 1984

ALIASES: Kevin Robert Burns, John Peter Daniel, Paul R. Burns, John William Pryor

DESCRIPTION

DATES OF BIRTH USED: October 30, 1948, November 3, 1948	**EYES:** Blue
PLACE OF BIRTH: Woodsville, New Hampshire	**SCARS, MARKS, TATTOOS:** None known.
HEIGHT: 5'7"	**SEX:** Male
WEIGHT: 150 lbs	**RACE:** White
OCCUPATION: Maintenance Man, Day Laborer	**NATIONALITY:** American
HAIR: Brown	**NCIC:** W856268298

REMARKS: Moses has a ruddy complexion.

CAUTION

On August 11, 1984, police were called to an apartment building in Joplin, Missouri, following an alleged burglary. While searching in and around the apartment complex, an officer discovered the body of a white female in a nearby vacant apartment that was undergoing renovation. Further investigation led authorities to Paul Allen Moses, a transient who was working as a day laborer at the apartment building where the body was found. A state arrest warrant was issued on August 11, 1984, charging Paul Allen Moses with capital murder. On March 21, 1995, a federal arrest warrant was issued in the Western District of Missouri, Springfield, Missouri, charging Moses with unlawful flight to avoid prosecution.

SHOULD BE CONSIDERED ARMED AND DANGEROUS

WANTED
FOR MURDER

DAVID NAM
REWARD

Unlawful flight to avoid prosecution – murder

WANTED BY THE FBI

Photograph taken in 1998

Photograph taken in 1997

ALIASES: David Heyon Nam, "Solid"

DESCRIPTION

DATE OF BIRTH: April 10, 1977
PLACE OF BIRTH: Norristown, Pennsylvania
HEIGHT: 6'1"
WEIGHT: 180 lbs
HAIR: Black
EYES: Brown

SCARS, MARKS, TATTOOS: Nam has the following tattoos: the word "NAM" on his right arm and the word "COBRA" on his back.
SEX: Male
RACE: Asian (Korean descent)
NATIONALITY: American

REMARKS: Nam speaks both English and Korean. He has ties to South Korea and may currently be residing there.

CAUTION

David Nam is wanted for his alleged involvement in the shooting death of an elderly man during a home invasion robbery in Philadelphia, Pennsylvania, on August 16, 1996. Nam was arrested for the murder on January 18, 1997, and subsequently released on bond pending trial. He failed to appear for his trial on March 12, 1998, and a warrant was issued for his arrest. A federal arrest warrant charging Nam with unlawful flight to avoid prosecution was then issued in the Eastern District of Pennsylvania on March 23, 1998. Further investigation by law enforcement officials determined that Nam had fled to South Korea and entered that country on March 13, 1998. Nam was subsequently arrested in South Korea on March 3, 1999, but released from custody because, at that time, no formal extradition treaty existed between the United States and South Korea. On December 20, 1999, a formal extradition agreement was ratified between the two nations. Nam, however, remains a fugitive.

SHOULD BE CONSIDERED ARMED AND DANGEROUS

WANTED
FOR MURDER

FRANCISCO JAVIER ROBLES

Wanted for first degree murder.

WANTED BY THE RENO, NEVADA POLICE DEPARTMENT

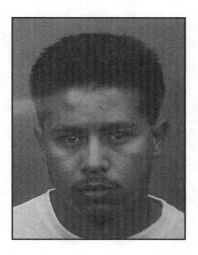

DESCRIPTION

DATES OF BIRTH USED: June 30, 1973	**EYES:** Brown	
PLACE OF BIRTH: China	**SEX:** Male	
HEIGHT: 5'7"	**RACE:** Mexican	
WEIGHT: 155 lbs	**WARRANT #:** 202791-96	
HAIR: Brown		

CAUTION

On September 8, 1996 Javier Robles Francisco became involved in an argument with Jose "Angel" Rodriguez-Castro in the parking lot of an apartment complex located at 1436 East Ninth Street in Reno, Nevada. During the argument Mr. Robles retreated briefly into a nearby apartment where he obtained a large caliber revolver. He returned to the parking lot and fired several shots which struck the victim who died as a result of his gunshot injuries. Immediately following the shooting Mr. Robles fled from Reno. Mr. Robles has family in San Jose, California, and in Mexico. His current whereabouts are unknown. A no bail arrest warrant has been issued charging Mr. Robles with 1st Degree Murder with a Deadly Weapon.

SHOULD BE CONSIDERED ARMED AND DANGEROUS

WANTED
MURDER

KUSHI SAMUELS

REWARD

WANTED BY THE ROYAL CANADIAN MOUNTED POLICE

DESCRIPTION

DATE OF BIRTH:	December 21, 1976	**EYES:**	Brown
HEIGHT:	5'6"	**SEX:**	Male
WEIGHT:	143 lbs	**RACE:**	Black
HAIR:	Black	**RCMP FILE #:**	95IP33710

CAUTION

In the early hours of April 22, 1995, at a rented reception hall in the St. Henri quarter of Montreal, a raucous, crowded birthday party was in progress. Throngs of young people, most of them members of the quarter's Jamaican community, danced and swayed to blaring reggae music.

As a pair of uninvited guests stealthily made their way through the crowd, two young revelers, Nicholas Rodriguez and Miguel Millings, headed for the exit. They recognized the intruders as associates of a local gang that supplied drugs to dealers in neighborhood schools. Police suspect the young men had had words prior to the party, perhaps over drug-dealing territory. No sooner had the two made it out to the sidewalk than one of the party crashers, 18-year-old Desta Barnes, followed them and opened fire. His accomplice, 18-year-old Kushi "K-G" Samuels, blocked the door and fired bullets into the crowd. Samuels then turned his attention to Millings and Rodriguez. In the end, 26-year-old Rodriguez was killed, 20-year-old Millings was left paralyzed for life from the waist down, and a 19-year-old bystander, Asher Manget, was wounded in the hand and knee.

Most of the shell casings at the scene were 6.35-mm, used in automatic weapons. There were also casings from a 9-mm Luger pistol. The evidence pointed to a gangland hit.

The shooters disappeared and police issued a nationwide alert for the two young murderers that witnesses identified as being natives of Jamaica and gang members. Samuels has not been seen since the night of the shooting. Desta Barnes, his partner in the brutal crime, was found dead in Miami almost a year later, his body riddled with bullets.

Samuels is thought to be in Montreal, Miami or Jamaica. He is considered armed and extremely dangerous.

WANTED

FOR MURDER

ALVIN SCOTT

REWARD

Unlawful flight to avoid prosecution – murder

WANTED BY THE FBI

ALIAS: Ahmet Sehsuvar

DESCRIPTION

DATES OF BIRTH USED: September 21, 1950; September 1, 1950	**EYES:** Brown
PLACE OF BIRTH: Turkey	**SCARS, MARKS, TATTOOS:** None known
HEIGHT: 6'0"	**SEX:** Male
WEIGHT: 170 lbs	**RACE:** White
OCCUPATION: Unknown	**NATIONALITY:** Turkish
HAIR: Gray	**NCIC:** W101821986

REMARKS: Scott is a naturalized citizen of the United States who may be traveling on a U.S. passport back to his native homeland of Turkey.

CAUTION

Alvin Scott is wanted in connection with the murder of his estranged wife and her male companion in the Buckhead area of Atlanta, Georgia, on August 3, 2001. Both victims were shot numerous times in both the torso and the head. On August 4, 2001, a City of Atlanta arrest warrant was issued for Scott. Then, on August 7, 2001, the United States District Court, Northern District of Georgia, issued a federal arrest warrant for Scott charging him with unlawful flight to avoid prosecution.

SHOULD BE CONSIDERED ARMED AND DANGEROUS

WANTED

FOR MURDER

WARREN STERN

REWARD

Unlawful flight to avoid prosecution – murder

WANTED BY THE FBI

ALIASES: Warren Sherman, "Ken," "Kenny," "Kenny Ken"

DESCRIPTION

DATE OF BIRTH USED: November 17 1970	**SCARS, MARKS, TATTOOS:** Stern has a tattoo on his right arm, possibly of the letters "WS."
PLACE OF BIRTH: South Africa	
HEIGHT: 5'11"	**SEX:** Male
WEIGHT: 170 lbs	**RACE:** White
OCCUPATION: Surf Shop Salesman	**NATIONALITY:** South African
HAIR: Brown	**NCIC :** W957817015
EYES: Blue	

REMARKS: Stern has ties to or may have traveled to Nevada, Utah, California, Mexico, England, and South Africa. Although he was born in South Africa, he grew up in West Los Angeles, California, and does not speak with an accent.

CAUTION

Warren Stern is wanted for the murder of a man in Santa Monica, California. On April 21, 1996, Stern was an uninvited guest at a birthday party for the victim. During the party, Stern allegedly got into a fight with the victim and stabbed him to death.

SHOULD BE CONSIDERED ARMED AND DANGEROUS

WANTED
FOR MURDER

DIEGO TREJO
REWARD

Unlawful flight to avoid prosecution – murder

WANTED BY THE FBI

ALIASES: Diego Trejo, Diego Trejo-Vasquez

DESCRIPTION

DATE OF BIRTH USED: November 30 1973
PLACE OF BIRTH: Hidalgo, Mexico
HEIGHT: 5'8"
WEIGHT: 145 lbs
OCCUPATION: Migrant Farm Worker, Employee at a Meat Processing Plant
HAIR: Black

EYES: Blue
SCARS, MARKS, TATTOOS: None known
SEX: Male
RACE: White (Hispanic)
NATIONALITY: Mexican
NCIC: W095175859

REMARKS: Trejo may have ties to Florida, North Carolina, and California.

CAUTION

Diego Trejo is wanted in connection with the murder of his wife, Pamela, who was stabbed to death during an altercation in their home in Alma, Georgia, on January 10, 1998. After taking his infant child to the home of a relative, Trejo fled the area. He is believed to be driving a tan, 1988 Ford F-150 pickup truck with Georgia license plates reading 8862RA. The license plates on the truck expired in 1998 and have not been renewed.

SHOULD BE CONSIDERED ARMED AND DANGEROUS

WANTED
MURDER

RICHARD VALLEE
$20,000 REWARD
WANTED BY U.S. MARSHALS

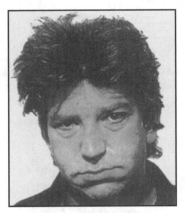

ALIAS: Richard Valley

DESCRIPTION

DATE OF BIRTH: November 10, 1957	**EYES:** Blue
PLACE OF BIRTH: Quebec	**SEX:** Male
HEIGHT: 5'10"	**RACE:** White
WEIGHT: 200 lbs	**SCARS/TATTOOS:** Unknown
HAIR: Brown	**NCIC#:** W007294002

CAUTION

Richard Vallee is wanted for the car bomb murder of a government informant named Lee Carter in Plattsburg, New York. The informant, Carter, was a part time bartender at a Bowl-Mart bowling alley when he was approached to smuggle cocaine into Canada For Richard Vallee, its ultimate buyer. As a result of Carters undercover work, Vallee was charged with cocaine trafficking.

Vallee retaliated with a bomb, which he placed in Carters car at the Bowl-Mart parking lot. As a result of this deed, Vallee was charged and convicted of Carters death. While awaiting extradition to the U.S. from Canada, Vallee devised a plan to break out of prison. He got into a fight and purposely had his jaw broken knowing that he would be taken to a hospital. Vallee escaped from Saint Lucs hospital on June 5, 1997 after subduing the security guard Vallee and his accomplice escaped on a motorcycle

Vallee is a member of the Hells Angels Nomads chapter of Montreal, and involved with a large-scale international cocaine smuggling organization. He speaks French and English, and is a computer science engineer. He is also trained in the use of explosives. He likes motorcycles, flashy jewelry and may be traveling with a girlfriend named Marie.

Unconfirmed reports have placed him in the Dominican Republic and the Netherlands. He is considered to be armed and dangerous. Report any information to the nearest U. S. Embassy, Consulate, or call The U.S. Marshal.

CONSIDERED ARMED AND DANGEROUS.

WANTED
FOR MURDER

KEVIN LOUIS VERMETTE
$17,500 REWARD
WANTED BY THE ROYAL CANADIAN MOUNTED POLICE

   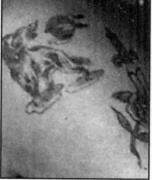

Tattoo on upper right arm   tattoo on upper left arm

DESCRIPTION

DATE OF BIRTH: November 18, 1954
HEIGHT: 5'9"
WEIGHT: 162 lbs
SCARS, MARKS, TATTOOS: Tattoo of "Cat" on upper right arm, with "Lucky" inscribed below, left upper arm "Coyote and Moon" and "Dagger through Red Rose"

OCCUPATION: Carpenter, Mechanical Knowledge, Truck Driver, Prefers Temporary Employment
HAIR: Brown
EYES: Blue
SEX: Male
RACE: White
NATIONALITY: Canadian
RCMP FILE: 97IP21528 (97-2149)

REMARKS: Clean shaven (at time of disappearance), and wears silver rimmed glasses.

CAUTION

A Canada wide warrant is outstanding for the above subject. He is believed to be responsible for the '97 July 12 triple shotgun murder of three innocent 20 year old youths which occurred in the northern community of Kitimat, British Columbia, Canada. He abandoned his vehicle at his motel residence and fled on foot into the mountain wilderness with his black lab dog. He may not be traveling with his dog at this time as he has a tendency to get rid of his dogs if they become undisciplined. Call your local Crimestoppers, local police department, or Kitimat RCMP, phone 250-632-7111. e-mail : rcmp@sno.net

SHOULD BE CONSIDERED ARMED AND DANGEROUS

WANTED
FOR MURDER

VINCENT LEGREND WALTERS

REWARD

Conspiracy to Manufacture and Possess with Intent to Distribute
888 Pounds of Methamphetamine

WANTED BY U.S. MARSHALS

ALIAS: "Tape"

DESCRIPTION

DATE OF BIRTH: December 10, 1966	**SCARS, MARKS, TATTOOS:** None known.
PLACE OF BIRTH: Mexico	**SEX:** Male
HEIGHT: 6'0"	**RACE:** White
WEIGHT: 170 lbs	**SCARS/TATTOOS:** Scar over left eye
HAIR: Brown	**SSN :** 524-85-2799
EYES: Brown	**NCIC:** W539479501
SKINTONE: Light Brown	

CAUTION

Walters has been indicted by the Bureau of Alcohol, Tobacco and Firearms for possession of a sawed-off shotgun. Walters is also wanted by the San Diego Police Department for homicide.

SHOULD BE CONSIDERED ARMED AND DANGEROUS

WANTED
DRUG SMUGGLING

JUAN CARLOS ARBOLEDA
REWARD

Subject leased a warehouse in the Baltimore area and formed a company as a front for a cocaine smuggling operation. Wanted for international drug smuggling (cocaine)

WANTED BY U.S. CUSTOMS

ALIAS: Juan Carlos

DESCRIPTION

DATE OF BIRTH: March 14, 1957	**SCARS, MARKS, TATTOOS:** None
PLACE OF BIRTH: Columbia	**HAIR:** Black
HEIGHT: 5'7"	**EYES:** Black
WEIGHT: 153 lbs	**COMPLEXION:** Medium
BUILD: Medium	**SEX:** Male
	RACE: Caucasian

In August 1996, the USCS Special Agent in Charge Baltimore, DEA Baltimore, FBI/Newark and the Baltimore City Police Department initiated the investigation of Chemical Treatment, Inc. The SAIC Baltimore investigation determined that the business was exporting large cylinders filled with chlorine gas to South America and then importing the empty cylinders as U.S. goods returned. The U.S. Customs Service Contraband Enforcement Team at the Port of Houston identified and examined a shipment of thirteen chlorine gas cylinders destined for the Baltimore warehouse. One of the cylinders was drilled and cocaine residue was discovered. When the cylinder was cut open, Customs agents discovered a large metal box concealed within the cylinder containing 164 kilograms of cocaine. Subsequent opening of the gas cylinders revealed that six of the thirteen cylinders contained a total of 1000 kilograms of cocaine. With the assistance of the Resident Agent in Charge Galveston, a controlled delivery was accomplished from Houston, Texas, to Chemical Treatment's warehouse in Baltimore, Maryland. The controlled delivery resulted in the arrests of three Colombian nationals who have since been found guilty. Juan Carlos Arboleda and Helena Munoz, the two individuals who were responsible for the organization and daily operation of the Chemical Treatment warehouse are believed to be in Colombia and remain U.S. Customs Fugitives. If you have any information regarding this fugitive contact the nearest U.S. Customs Office or call the U.S. Customs National Law Enforcement Center at 1-800-BE ALERT.

WANTED
FOR DRUG DISTRIBUTION

ANDREAS CAMACHO JR.

REWARD

Import and possession with intent to distribute methaqualone

WANTED BY U.S. MARSHALS SERVICE

ALIASES: none

DESCRIPTION

DATE OF BIRTH: November 1, 1956	EYES: Brown
PLACE OF BIRTH: Columbia	SCARS, MARKS, TATTOOS: Unknown
HEIGHT: 5'6"	SEX: Male
WEIGHT: 180 lbs	RACE: White
HAIR: Brown	NCIC #: W382007422

CAUTION

Camacho was arrested by local authorities in Okeechobee county, FL, on 4/28/81 for trafficking in methaqualone. In 1982 he was indicted by a Northern Florida federal grand jury for conspiracy to possess with intent to distribute methaqualone. He was never arrested on this charge. In 1985 the Southern Florida federal grand jury indicted Camacho for importation of methaqualone, and conspiracy to possess with intent to distribute methaqualone. He was never arrested on that indictment either. It is believed that Camacho fled to his homeland of Colombia. However, information has been developed that Camacho maintains contact with relatives in the Miami area. He possibly has adopted a new identity in order to travel to the U.S. undetected.

CONSIDERED ARMED AND DANGEROUS.

WANTED
DRUG DISTRIBUTION

CHANG CHI-FU
$2,000,000 REWARD

WANTED BY THE BUREAU FOR INTERNATIONAL NARCOTICS AND LAW ENFORCEMENT AFFAIRS

ALIAS: Khun Sa

DESCRIPTION

DATES OF BIRTH USED: February 17, 1933 and February 12, 1932	**HAIR:** Black
PLACE OF BIRTH: Loi Maw, Burma	**EYES:** Brown
HEIGHT: 5'10"	**SEX:** Male
WEIGHT: 150 lbs	**RACE:** Asian
	NATIONALITY: Burmese

CAUTION

Chang Chi-Fu is the former head of the Shan United Army (SUA), also known as the Mong Thai Army (MTA), which was a dominant force in Southeast Asia's narcotics trade and the world's largest producer of heroin prior to capitulating to the government of Burma in 1996. Chang Chi-Fu is wanted on Federal drug violations in the Eastern District of New York that included conspiracy, importation of, and possession with intent to distribute heroin in the United States. He is believed to be residing in a military safe house in Rangoon, Burma, under a cease fire and amnesty agreement with the Burmese Government. The U.S. Department of State is offering a reward of up to $2,000,000 for information leading to the arrest or conviction in the United States of Chang Chi-Fu. If you have information, and you are outside the United States, please contact the nearest U.S. Embassy or Consulate. In the United States, please contact the Federal Bureau of Investigation (FBI), or DEA office in your city.

WANTED
FOR DRUG DISTRIBUTION

TRAVIS S. DUNN

REWARD

Distribution of hallucinogens, LSD

WANTED BY U.S. MARSHALS SERVICE

 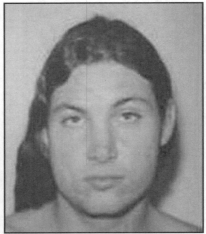 

ALIASES: Travis Rainwater, Ray Park, John Travis Nelson, Bongo Boy Dunn, the "Hippie"

DESCRIPTION

DATE OF BIRTH: November 12, 1970	**EYES:** Brown
PLACE OF BIRTH: South Carolina	**SCARS, MARKS, TATTOOS:** Unknown
HEIGHT: 6'2"	**SEX:** Male
WEIGHT: 180 lbs	**RACE:** White
HAIR: Brown	**NCIC #:** W136788772

CAUTION

Dunn left Vermont in February, 1999 and is an avid follower of the Rainbow group. He distributes LSD in the form of gelcaps. Dunn was last seen in Brattleboro VT when he was arrested with a large quantity of LSD. Subject may possibly be with members of the Rainbow Group. According to the Department of Motor Vehicles, DUNN has a Red GMC Van VT reg CBP440 or VT reg CAP456. Dunn has been known to frequent college campuses. Subject reportedly carries a concealed knife.

CONSIDERED ARMED AND DANGEROUS.

WANTED
FOR DRUG SMUGGLING

DAVID GARZON-ANGUIANO
REWARD

International Drug Smuggling (Cocaine)

WANTED BY U.S. CUSTOMS

DESCRIPTION

DATE OF BIRTH: July 26, 1972
PLACE OF BIRTH: Ciudad Obregon, Sonora, Mexico
HEIGHT: 5'11"
WEIGHT: 200 lbs
HAIR: Brown
EYES: Brown

COMPLEXION: Medium
SCARS, MARKS, TATTOOS: Scar from appendectomy
SEX: Male
RACE: Latin
WARRANT NUMBER: W034578228 / 97CR2102N

CAUTION

On June 16, 1997, David Garzon-Anguiano was indicted by a Federal Grand Jury on charges related to Smuggling and Possession with the Intent to Distribute Cocaine into the United States in violation of Title 21 United States Code, Sections 841, 846, 952, 960, and 963. Garzon-Anguiano drove a 1995 Oldsmobile with California license plate 2BSK558 to the Port of Entry in Calexico, CA. Garzon-Anguiano was ordered to open the trunk of the vehicle for inspection. Both Garzon-Anguiano and the passenger, Lazaro Beltran fled the area and ran back to Mexico on foot. The abandoned vehicle was laden with 923 pounds of Cocaine unconcealed in the trunk. Garzon-Anguiano still continues his drug smuggling activities and is continuing to "climb up" the Arellano-Felix Drug Trafficking Organization. At this time, Garzon-Anguiano remains a fugitive and may reside in Mexicali, Baja California, Mexico.

CONSIDERED ARMED AND DANGEROUS.

WANTED
FOR DRUG SMUGGLING, MURDER

GERALD LYLE HEMP

REWARD

HEMP has been implicated in three homicides. HEMP was serving a
40-year sentence when he escaped.

WANTED BY U.S. MARSHALS SERVICE

ALIASES: Jerry Whittier, James Comstock, George Baker

DESCRIPTION

DATE OF BIRTH: September 5, 1934
PLACE OF BIRTH: Peoria, Illinois
HEIGHT: 5'11"
WEIGHT: 220 lbs
HAIR: Brown
EYES: Blue
SKIN TONE: Fair

SCARS, MARKS, TATTOOS: One-inch scar on right side of right eye. Tattoos: Airborne Ranger, Geisha Girl, Rose.
SEX: Male
SSN: 359-28-8147
NCIC #: W443684869

CAUTION

Gerald Lyle Hemp was convicted in 1984 of smuggling six hundred kilograms of cocaine into the U.S. He was sentenced to forty years in prison. On November 5th, 1986, while serving his sentence in a Florida prison, he was indicted on racketeering charges. The next day, he escaped. Hemp has also been implicated in three murders. Authorities believe he has fled U.S. jurisdiction.

CONSIDERED ARMED AND DANGEROUS. DO NOT ATTEMPT TO APPREHEND THIS PERSON YOURSELF. REPORT ANY INFORMATION TO THE NEAREST USMS DISTRICT OFFICE.

WANTED
DRUG DISTRIBUTION

WEI HSUEH-KANG
$2,000,000 REWARD

WANTED BY THE BUREAU FOR INTERNATIONAL NARCOTICS AND LAW ENFORCEMENT AFFAIRS

ALIAS: Prasit Chivinnitipanya

DESCRIPTION

DATE OF BIRTH USED: May 19, 1952	**EYES:** Brown
PLACE OF BIRTH: China	**SEX:** Male
HEIGHT: 5'6"	**RACE:** Asian
WEIGHT: 125 lbs	**NATIONALITY:** Chinese
HAIR: Black	

CAUTION

Wei Hsueh-Kang, the commander of the United WA State Army's (UWSA or WA) Southern Military Command, is wanted on Federal drug violations in the Eastern District of New York. The WA is currently the dominant heroin trafficking group in Southeast Asia, and possibly worldwide. Wei Hsueh-Kang is believed to be in hiding in Burma. The U.S. Department of State is offering a reward of up to $2,000,000 for information leading to the arrest or conviction in the United States of Wei Hsueh-Kang. If you have information, and you are outside the United States, please contact the nearest U.S. Embassy or Consulate. In the United States, please contact the Federal Bureau of Investigation (FBI), or DEA office in your city.

WANTED
DRUG DISTRIBUTION

SIDNEY MARVIN LEWIS

REWARD

Lewis' original charge was possession with intent to distribute 25 tons of hashish. Lewis is associated with organized crime and is known to be heavily armed.

WANTED BY U.S. MARSHALS & U.S CUSTOMS

ALIAS: Sid Shajbra

DESCRIPTION

DATE OF BIRTH: September 13, 1937	**SCARS, MARKS, TATTOOS:** Light scar & pox on left cheek
PLACE OF BIRTH: Chicago, Illinois	**COMPLEXION:** Medium
HEIGHT: 5'10"	**SEX:** Male
WEIGHT: 180 lbs	**RACE:** Caucasian
BUILD: Medium	**NCIC:** W568098909
HAIR: Gray	
EYES: Blue	

CAUTION

In September 1989, an attempt to off-load 25 tons of hashish from the Motor Vessel Lady Brigid in Columbia City, Oregon, was unsuccessful. The 25 tons of hashish, the Motor Vessel lady Brigid and related vehicles were seized, and seven people were arrested. The investigation revealed that Sidney Lewis was the owner and master of the Lady Brigid. Lewis should be considered armed and dangerous and is a U.S. Customs Fugitive. If you have any information regarding this fugitive contact the nearest U.S. Customs Office or call the U.S. Customs National Law Enforcement Center at 1-800-BE ALERT.

SHOULD BE CONSIDERED ARMED AND DANGEROUS

WANTED
FOR DRUG DISTRIBUTION

EDWARD MATHIS

REWARD

Wanted for Narcotics Violations

WANTED BY U.S. MARSHALS SERVICE

ALIASES: Eddie Whitson, John Whitson, Eddie Mathis, "Lucky"

DESCRIPTION

DATE OF BIRTH: November 12, 1963	**SCARS, MARKS, TATTOOS:** Tattoo left arm
PLACE OF BIRTH: New Jersey	**COMPLEXION:** Fair
HEIGHT: 5'9"	**SEX:** Male
WEIGHT: 190 lbs	**RACE:** Hispanic
HAIR: Black	**SSN:** 098-60-7956
EYES: Brown	**NCIC #:** W988196342

CAUTION

Mathis has been implicated as the triggerman in a double homicide using a MAC-10 machine gun with silencer in the Eastern District of New York. He was a co-leader and enforcer for a crack ring on Long Island, NY, and is wanted for conspiracy to distribute cocaine and crack cocaine.

CONSIDERED ARMED AND DANGEROUS. DO NOT ATTEMPT TO APPREHEND THIS PERSON YOURSELF. REPORT ANY INFORMATION TO THE NEAREST USMS DISTRICT OFFICE.

WANTED
FOR DRUG SMUGGLING

FRANCIS MOULAN

REWARD

Wanted for International Drug Smuggling (Cocaine)

WANTED BY U.S. CUSTOMS

ALIAS: Francis Moulan Miller

DESCRIPTION

DATE OF BIRTH: July 9, 1969
PLACE OF BIRTH: Dominica
HEIGHT: 5'11"
WEIGHT: 195 lbs
HAIR: Black
EYES: Brown

SCARS, MARKS, TATTOOS: Unknown, however is missing a finger on right hand
SKIN TONE: Unknown
SEX: Male
WARRANT #: 992103190733-J

CAUTION

On March 15, 1999, a warrant for arrest was issued for Francis Moulan for conspiracy to violate Title 21 United States Code, Section 963 (Conspiracy to Distribute and Possession with Intent to Distribute Cocaine and Cocaine Base). Moulan is the partner of the leader of the "Island Boys" drug smuggling organization. Moulan is linked to a seizure of over 1260 kilograms of cocaine which was intercepted on the island of Tortola, British Virgin Islands. A shootout resulted and a Tortolan police officer was seriously wounded. The subject was recognized by other Tortolan police officers at the scene, but Moulan was able to escape apprehension. Moulan is believed to and should be considered Armed and Dangerous.

WANTED
FOR DRUG SMUGGLING

JOHN INNOCENT OKAFOR

REWARD

Wanted for International Narcotics Smuggling (Cocaine)

WANTED BY U.S. CUSTOMS

ALIAS: Jefferey Anderson

DESCRIPTION

DATE OF BIRTH: September 10, 1962	**SCARS, MARKS, TATTOOS:** None
PLACE OF BIRTH: Onitsha, Nigeria	**EYES:** Brown
HEIGHT: 5'11"	**COMPLEXION:** Dark
WEIGHT: 180 lbs	**SEX:** Male
HAIR: Brown	**WARRANT #:** W75140038

CAUTION

In March 1991, U.S. Customs seized over a Kilo of heroin from a heroin courier for John Innocent Okafor's heroin smuggling organization. The courier was traveling from Singapore via Tokyo, Japan, to New York. Customs developed leads and forwarded the leads to Japanese authorities and two more couriers were arrested in Japan transporting heroin for Okafor. In April 1991, a warrant for the arrest of Okafor was issued charging him with violation of Title 21 United States Code Sections 952, 960, and 963, Conspiracy to possess with Intent to Distribute Heroin and Conspiracy to Import Heroin into the United States.

WANTED
FOR DRUG DISTRIBUTION

ISRAEL RODRIGUEZ

REWARD

Wanted for Federal Drug Violations

WANTED BY THE BUREAU OF ALCOHOL, TOBACCO AND FIREARMS

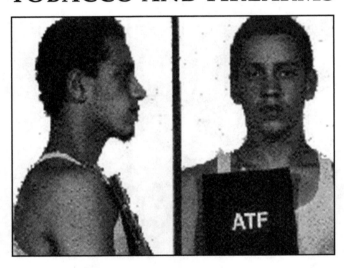

ALIASES: Pito Rodriguez, Issie Rodriguez, Israel Vega

DESCRIPTION

DATE OF BIRTH: August 4, 1968	**EYES:** Brown
PLACE OF BIRTH: New York	**COMPLEXION:** Medium
HEIGHT: 5'8"	**SEX:** Male
WEIGHT: 140 lbs	**RACE:** Hispanic
BUILD: Medium	**NATIONALITY:** American
HAIR: Brown	**FEDERAL WARRANT #:** 706534552

CAUTION

Israel Rodriguez is wanted for conspiracy to distribute narcotics and use of handguns during narcotics trafficking. Rodriguez possessed a short barreled shotgun, 2 handguns and 2 kilo's of crack cocaine on his last arrest. Rodriguez is known to travel to New York and Puerto Rico.

WANTED
FOR DRUG SMUGGLING

LIU SZU-PO
$2,000,000 REWARD

International drug smuggling – cocaine

WANTED BY THE BUREAU FOR INTERNATIONAL NARCOTICS AND LAW ENFORCEMENT AFFAIRS, U.S. DEPARTMENT OF STATE

ALIASES: Damrat Namsuwakhon, Lamdap Namsuwakhon

DESCRIPTION

DATE OF BIRTH:	1952	**EYES:**	Dark
PLACE OF BIRTH:	Thailand	**SKIN TONE:**	Light
HEIGHT:	5'4"	**SEX:**	Male
WEIGHT:	155 lbs	**RACE:**	Asian
HAIR:	Black	**NATIONALITY:**	Thai

CAUTION

Liu Szu-Po is wanted in the Eastern District of New York for Federal drug violations of importation of heroin into the United States, attempted heroin importation and conspiracy. He was a principal heroin distributor for Chang Chi-Fu and now operates several heroin refineries along the border of Thailand and Burma north of Chiang Rai Province, Thailand. He has been hiding in Mong Kan, Sheh Pi and Wan Chang in Burma, and was last seen in Thailand at Ban Hin Taek (Chiang Rai) where he maintains a large residence. The U.S. Department of State is offering a reward of up to $2,000,000 for information leading to the arrest or conviction in the United States of Liu Szu-Po.

CONSIDERED ARMED AND DANGEROUS.

WANTED

FOR DRUG SMUGGLING

ROBERT ANTHONY WALKER

REWARD

International drug smuggling – cocaine

WANTED BY U.S. CUSTOMS

ALIASES: Ralph Newman (real name), Colin James, Preston LNU, Rusty LNU

DESCRIPTION

DATE OF BIRTH:	November 2, 1971	**EYES:**	Brown
PLACE OF BIRTH:	St. James, Jamaica	**SKIN TONE:**	Light
HEIGHT:	6'1"	**SCARS, MARKS, TATTOOS:**	Unknown
WEIGHT:	225 lbs	**SEX:**	Male
HAIR:	Black	**RACE:**	Black
		WARRANT #:	6:01-CR-34-ORL-19KRS

CAUTION

In February, 2001, Robert Anthony Walker was indicted in the Middle District of Florida, charging him with conspiracy to import a controlled substance (cocaine) in violation of Title 21 United States Code, Section 963. On March 13, 2001, a Federal arrest warrant was issued for Robert Anthony Walker from the Middle District of Florida. Walker also has a Federal bench warrant for his arrest issued from the Southern District of Florida for violation of his probation. Walker is the leader of a cocaine smuggling organization and is responsible for the importation of at least 100 kilograms of cocaine smuggled from Jamaica and distributed to Central and Southern Florida during the last three years. Walker is a Jamaican National and his last known address is 4760 NW 24th Court #B116, Lauderdale Lakes, Florida.

CONSIDERED ARMED AND DANGEROUS.

WANTED

FOR SEXUAL ASSAULT

STEVEN RANDALL ARTHUR

REWARD

Unlawful flight to avoid prosecution – aggravated criminal sexual assault

WANTED BY THE FBI

ALIAS: Steven R. Arthur, "Goober"

DESCRIPTION

DATE OF BIRTH USED: December 4, 1959	**SEX:** Male
PLACE OF BIRTH: West Virginia	**RACE:** White
HEIGHT: 5'11"	**OCCUPATIONS:** Carnival vendor, fruit picker, car salesman
WEIGHT: 220 lbs	
HAIR: Black	**NATIONALITY:** American
EYES: Brown	**NCIC #:** W763828395
SCARS, MARKS: None known	

REMARKS: Arthur has ties to West Virginia and Florida. He is believed to have traveled with carnivals in the past, working for the vendor companies. At the time of his disappearance, Arthur was believed to be suicidal.

CAUTION

It is alleged that between 1991 and 1993, Steven Randall Arthur had repeated sexual contact with several young girls while they were being babysat in his residence in Hutsonville, Illinois. After authorities became aware of his alleged activities, Arthur decided to leave Illinois in July of 1993 before he could be arrested. On July 29, 1993, a state arrest warrant was issued in the Second Judicial District, Crawford County, Illinois, charging Arthur with aggravated criminal sexual assault. On August 30, 1993, a federal arrest warrant was issued in the Southern District of Illinois, East St. Louis, Illinois, charging Arthur with unlawful flight to avoid prosecution.

WANTED
AGGRAVATED SEXUAL ASSAULT

JAMES BYRON CARLSON
REWARD
Unlawful flight to avoid prosecution – AGGRAVATED SEXUAL ASSAULT
WANTED BY THE FBI

ALIASES: James B Carlson, Jim Carlson

DESCRIPTION

DATE OF BIRTH: April 19, 1941
PLACE OF BIRTH: Texas
HEIGHT: 6'1"
WEIGHT: 200 lbs
HAIR: Brown/Gray
EYES: Brown
SEX: Male
RACE: White

SCARS, MARKS, TATTOOS: Carlson has tattoos on his right upper arm, and right wrist. He also has scars on both hands from chemical burns.
NATIONALITY: American
NCIC #: W133193407
OCCUPATIONS: Mechanic, truck driver, roughneck (oil-well crew member)

REMARKS: James Byron Carlson is believed to be with his wife Dorothy Dee Carlson, who is also a fugitive. He is a skilled mechanic and used to drive a tractor trailer for a living. He may have also worked in sales in the past and enjoys woodworking as a hobby.

CAUTION
In September of 1995, local authorities in Bastrop County, Texas, obtained felony arrest warrants for James Byron Carlson and his wife Dorothy Dee Carlson. James Carlson was charged with sexual assault of a child and Dorothy Carlson was charged with sexual performance of a child. After being arrested and later found guilty in a jury trial, James Carlson was freed on bond. An indictment was also returned against Dorothy Carlson on charges of sexual performance of a child. When neither of them appeared in court for their next scheduled appearances, James Carlson was sentenced to 99 years of incarceration in his absence, and Dorothy Carlson was charged with failure to appear.

CONSIDERED ARMED AND DANGEROUS.

WANTED
AGGRAVATED SEXUAL ASSAULT

DOROTHY DEE CARLSON
REWARD

Unlawful flight to avoid prosecution – AGGRAVATED SEXUAL ASSAULT

WANTED BY THE FBI

ALIASES: Dorothy Dee Carlson

DESCRIPTION

DATE OF BIRTH: May 11, 1959	SEX: Female
PLACE OF BIRTH: Unknown	RACE: White
HEIGHT: 5'4"	SCARS, MARKS, TATTOOS: None known
WEIGHT: 125 lbs	NATIONALITY: American
HAIR: Blonde	NCIC #: W133196110
EYES: Blue	OCCUPATIONS: Waitress

REMARKS: Dorothy Dee Carlson is believed to be with her husband, James Byron Carlson, who is also a fugitive.

CAUTION

In September of 1995, local authorities in Bastrop County, Texas, obtained felony arrest warrants for Dorothy Dee Carlson and her husband James Byron Carlson. Dorothy Dee Carlson was charged with sexual performance of a child and James Carlson was charged with sexual assault of a child. After their arrests, an indictment was returned against Dorothy Carlson on charges of sexual performance of a child. James Carlson was later found guilty in a jury trial and freed on bond. When neither of them appeared in court for their next scheduled appearances, Dorothy Carlson was charged with failure to appear and James Carlson was sentenced to 99 years of incarceration in his absence.

CONSIDERED ARMED AND DANGEROUS.

WANTED
FOR SEXUAL ASSAULT

ANDREW ALLBRITTON, JR.

WANTED BY THE FBI

DESCRIPTION

DATE OF BIRTH: January 1, 1934
PLACE OF BIRTH: Wisner, Louisiana
HEIGHT: 6' 1"
WEIGHT: 200 pounds
OCCUPATIONS: Former farmer/rancher
SCARS AND MARKS: He has a scar on his nose.

HAIR: Gray
EYES: Hazel
RACE: White
SEX: Male
NATIONALITY: American

REMARKS: Allbritton has chronic lung problems due to heavy smoking and requires periodic medical treatment. Allbritton likes western-style clothes and enjoys horseback riding. He may be in Reynosa, Mexico. He was last known to be driving a blue 1994 Ford pick-up truck with Louisiana license plates, number S493955.

DETAILS

Andrew Allbritton, Jr., is wanted for sexually molesting his eight-year-old grand-daughter in Wisner, Louisiana. On January 18th, 1996, the child's mother left the child in Allbritton's care for one night. It was during this time that the crime occurred. Several days later, the child told her parents about the molestation. After an examination by a physician, an investigation was made by local law enforcement authorities. Allbritton was arrested and charged with aggravated incest. Released on bond, Allbritton failed to appear in court for trial in October 1997. A federal warrant was issued for his arrest for unlawful flight to avoid prosecution. He is believed to have fled U.S. jurisdiction.

WANTED

DISTRIBUTION OF CHILD PORNOGRAPHY

DAVID CREAMER

REWARD

International distribution of child pornography

WANTED BY U.S. MARSHALS SERVICE

ALIASES: David Ben Creamer, Dave Creamer, Benjamin Creamer David

DESCRIPTION

DATE OF BIRTH: July 19, 1946	**SKINTONE:** Light
PLACE OF BIRTH: Tucson, Arizona	**SCARS, MARKS, TATTOOS:** Scars on upper lip, right leg, right knee. Wears glasses.
HEIGHT: 5'10"	
WEIGHT: 230 lbs	**SEX:** Male
HAIR: Brown	**RACE:** White
EYES: Blue	**WARRANT #:** WO48242928

CAUTION

In April 1993, the Special Agent in Charge Tucson initiated an investigation regarding bulletin board services (bbs) sales, and sales of CD/ROM diskettes containing adult obscenity, bestiality and child pornography. The distributor was identified as Profit Group, in Ft. Lowell, Tucson, Arizona. The investigation revealed that the chief corporate officers were David Creamer and Shirley Thompson. Creamer was indicted in December 1997, and remains a U.S. Customs Fugitive.

CONSIDERED ARMED AND DANGEROUS.

WANTED
FOR SEXUAL ASSAULT

WILFRED ERNEST ELDER

REWARD

Wanted for: Aggravated Sexual Assault, Sexual Assault with a Weapon, Unlawful Confinement, Utter Threats, Parole Revocation

WANTED BY THE ROYAL CANADIAN MOUNTED POLICE

DESCRIPTION

DATE OF BIRTH: April 4, 1957	HAIR: Brown
PLACE OF BIRTH: Saskatchewan, Canada	EYES: Brown
HEIGHT: 6'1"	SEX: Male
WEIGHT: 180 lbs	RACE: White
SCARS, MARKS, TATTOOS: Left upper arm (Phoenix bird), right upper arm (knife, girl with glasses)	NATIONALITY: Canadian
	RCMP FILE: 2000IP64179 Merit (BC)

CAUTION

Wilfred Ernest Elder is a suspect in two sexual assaults occurring in Merritt, British Columbia in January/February 1998. Also wanted for Federal Parole violations.

SHOULD BE CONSIDERED ARMED AND DANGEROUS

International Crime Alert
WILFRED ERNEST ELDER

In the middle of the night on Wednesday, February 11, 1998, Julie Simmons awoke to a pounding on her door. Simmons, a 25-year-old single mother, lived in a quiet residential area in Merritt, a town of about 8,000 in British Columbia's southern interior.

When she opened the door, Simmons was greeted by her friend and neighbor from across the street, 24-year-old John Balsam. With Balsam was a big, rough-looking man with long dark hair and a mustache. Balsam introduced the man as Butch. The two were in a partying mood.

Balsam and Butch had beer with them, and after a few drinks in the living room, they suggested that the three of them go out somewhere. But Simmons' two-year-old son was sleeping upstairs, so she asked the men to leave. Balsam did, but Butch was adamant about staying a little longer.

Wilfred "Butch" Elder

AGE: 43
HEIGHT: 6'1"
WEIGHT: 180 lbs.
EYES: Brown
HAIR: Brown
CONTACT: RCMP in Merritt, B.C., at 250-378-4262; or your local police.

Simmons was soon uncomfortable. The burly, tattooed man seemed edgy and preoccupied, and watched her like a snake. After about 20 minutes of chugging beer and making small talk, Butch moved next to Simmons on the couch and began to paw her. "Could you please go?" Simmons demanded, trying to fend him off. But the big man was relentless; soon he had a hand about her throat and was ripping her clothes off.

Butch sexually assaulted Simmons, then threatened that he would kill her if she told anyone. But Simmons phoned the police immediately after he left, and the Merritt RCMP responded within minutes. Butch was nowhere to be found.

A few days later another woman, who had heard of the incident, told Merritt RCMP that she, too, had been sexually assaulted by Butch the previous month.

Butch's real name is Wilfred Ernest Elder. He acquired the nickname Butch in his native Saskatchewan and was known by that name while with the Hells Angels in Vancouver.

Elder was born on the Little Quill Reserve (formerly Nut Lake Reserve). He is fair complexioned, with Caucasian features. He has spent a total of 17 years in prison for sexual assaults and other violent offenses across Canada, including attempted kidnapping in Calgary in 1978.

An unconfirmed sighting of Elder was reported in North Battleford, Sask., in July 1999. Authorities say he may have changed his appearance by cutting his hair and shaving. He has an ex-wife and a son in Kelowna, B.C.

Elder likes to fraternize with members of biker gangs and to drink in strip clubs, in which he has frequently worked as a bouncer. He fancies himself a native artist and likes to proselytize on First Nations' rights. He may be in Vancouver, Kelowna, Kamloops, B.C., or North Battleford; he has family, friends and former associates in most of those places.

Elder assaults women he barely knows by catching them alone and then choking them or holding a knife to their throat. He usually threatens them with death should they go to the police. The man is dangerous and if seen should be reported to your local police.

WANTED

FOR INDECENT ACTS WITH A CHILD

HAROLD RUSSELL FINBERG

REWARD

Sodomy, indecent acts with a child, desertion

WANTED BY THE NAVAL CRIMINAL INVESTIGATIVE SERVICE

DESCRIPTION

DATE OF BIRTH: September 10, 1965	**SCARS, MARKS, TATTOOS:** None known
PLACE OF BIRTH: New Mexico	**SEX:** Male
HEIGHT: 5'6"	**RACE:** White
WEIGHT: 170 lbs	**NATIONALITY:** American
HAIR: Brown	**NCIS CASE #:** 08DEC97-HIHN-0445-7FNA
EYES: Hazel	**OCCUPATION:** Navy Yeoman

REMARKS: Sometimes wears a mustache and has been known to wear military style glasses.

CAUTION

Second Class Yeoman Harold Russell Finberg, who deserted Dec. 5, 1997, from Pearl Harbor while awaiting court-martial for allegedly assaulting and taking indecent liberties with a minor, is believed to still be in the islands. Finberg was later convicted of one charge of sodomy and two charges of indecent acts with a minor. He was sentenced to a prison term of seven years, given a dishonorable discharge and fined forfeiture of pay and allowance of $900 per month for seven years. Assigned to the staff of the commander in chief of the Pacific before he deserted, Finberg is 5 feet 6 inches tall, weighs 170 pounds and has brown hair. Anyone having information may call Naval Criminal Investigative Service at (800) 474-1218.

CONSIDERED ARMED AND DANGEROUS.

WANTED

FOR SEXUAL BATTERY

EDWARD EUGENE HARPER

REWARD

Unlawful flight to avoid prosecution – conspiracy to commit sexual battery, fondling, sexual battery

WANTED BY THE FBI

 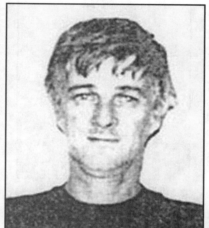 

ALIASES: Edward E. Harper, Ed E. Harper, Eddie Eugene Trimue, Eddie Harper, Eddie Eugene Harper, Edward Eugene Trimue, Ed Harmon

DESCRIPTION

DATE OF BIRTH: March 1, 1946	**SCARS, MARKS, TATTOOS:** None known
PLACE OF BIRTH: New Mexico	**SEX:** Male
HEIGHT: 5'10"	**RACE:** White
WEIGHT: 165 lbs	**NATIONALITY:** American
HAIR: Gray/Brown	**NCIC #:** W134456931
EYES: Hazel	**OCCUPATIONS:** Semi-truck driver, mechanic, forklift driver, ranch handler,

REMARKS: Harper considers himself to be a member of the Freemen Sovereign Citizen Group. He has family ties in Arkansas. It is believed he has been doing ranching work in Montana and Wyoming.

CAUTION

Edward Eugene Harper is wanted for allegedly having sexual relations with a child under the age of fourteen in Hernando, Mississippi. On April 27, 1994, a state arrest warrant was issued by the Circuit Court of DeSoto County, Mississippi, charging Harper with conspiracy to commit sexual battery, child fondling and sexual battery. A federal arrest warrant was subsequently obtained in the Northern District of Mississippi, charging Harper with unlawful flight to avoid prosecution.

CONSIDERED ARMED AND DANGEROUS.

WANTED
RAPE

RAYMOND E. JONES
REWARD
Unlawful flight to avoid prosecution – rape
WANTED BY THE FBI

ALIASES: Ray Jones, Joey Jones, Randy Jones, Raymond Ernest Jones, Raymond Earnest Jones

DESCRIPTION

DATE OF BIRTH: August 8, 1966	RACE: White
PLACE OF BIRTH: Durant, Mississippi	SCARS, MARKS, TATTOOS: None known
HEIGHT: 5'10"	NATIONALITY: Canadian
WEIGHT: 225 lbs	NCIC #: W990323884
HAIR: Dirty/Sandy Blond	OCCUPATIONS: Nurse (Obstetrics/Gynecology),
EYES: Blue	Certified Emergency Medical Technician, Sales Clerk
SEX: Male	

REMARKS: Jones is reportedly very neat, meticulous and organized. Jones was in the Air Force from 1985 to 1989, and later became a member of the Mississippi Air National Guard. He has resided in Grenada, Mississippi, and at an Air Force Base in Wichita, Kansas. He has reportedly expressed interest in traveling to Australia, Canada, and Germany.

CAUTION

Raymond E. Jones is wanted for allegedly raping a minor female for approximately six years in Grenada, Mississippi. In October of 1996, authorities in Mississippi discovered that the victim had been sexually assaulted. At the time the crime was discovered, Jones was away from his home in Mississippi attending an Air Force training school in Texas. A local warrant was soon obtained for the arrest of Jones on three counts of rape. However, Jones did not return to Mississippi after his training in Texas. Then, in March of 1997, a federal arrest warrant was issued in the Northern District of Mississippi charging Jones with unlawful flight to avoid prosecution. In February of 1999, Jones reportedly appeared at the victim's place of employment, a restaurant in Mississippi. However, Jones remains at large.

CONSIDERED ARMED AND DANGEROUS.

WANTED
FOR SEXUAL ASSAULT

PATTY ANN KENLEY

Unlawful flight to avoid prosecution – aggravated sexual assault of a child

WANTED BY FBI

ALIAS: Pattyann Hutson Kenley

DESCRIPTION

DATE OF BIRTH: April 6, 1968
PLACE OF BIRTH: Unknown
HEIGHT: 5'8"
WEIGHT: 200 lbs
HAIR: Brown
EYES: Blue

SCARS, MARKS, TATTOOS: Kenley has a small scar on her left buttocks and a scar on her right leg.
SEX: Female
RACE: White
NATIONALITY: Unknown
NCIC #: W820111195

REMARKS: Kenley is believed to be with her husband, Phillip J. Kenley, who is also a fugitive. They may have ties to Springville, Arkansas.

CAUTION

In June of 1997, allegations of sexual assault were made by a minor child to local authorities in Collin County, Texas. The eleven-year-old boy alleged that between April and June of 1997, his stepmother, Patty Ann Kenley, sexually assaulted him in the presence of his father, Phillip J Kenley, and a younger sister. Arrest warrants were issued for Patty and Phillip Kenley on June 13, 1997. That day, the Kenleys were both arrested in Colin County, Texas, and posted bond. The Kenleys then failed to appear for their scheduled court date, resulting in the forfeiture of their bonds. On August 25, 1999, federal arrest warrants were issued in Sherman, Texas, charging Patty Ann Kenley and Phillip J. Kenley with unlawful flight to avoid prosecution.

CONSIDERED ARMED AND DANGEROUS.

WANTED
MAILING OF OBSCENE MATERIAL

MYRON HERBERT SHAPIRO
REWARD

Mailing of obscene material and unlawful flight to avoid prosecution

WANTED BY U.S. POSTAL INSPECTION

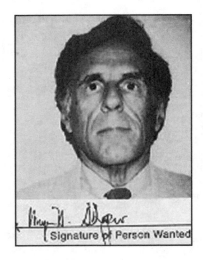

Signature of Person Wanted

DESCRIPTION

DATE OF BIRTH: May 8. 1926	**SEX:** Male
PLACE OF BIRTH: New York	**RACE:** White
HEIGHT: 5'11"	**SCARS, MARKS, TATTOOS:** None known
WEIGHT: 168 lbs	**NATIONALITY:** American
HAIR: Brown	**WARRANT #:** 9167-0409-0042-B
EYES: Brown	**OCCUPATION:** Self-employed businessman

CAUTION

Myron Herbert Shapiro is a white male, born in the state of New York on May 8 or 9, 1926. He has a medium build and may wear reading glasses. He speaks English only and may represent himself as a retired businessman. He is traveling on a U.S. passport, number 042158770, issued May 27, 1988. His wife, Carol Lee Shapiro, also known as Barbara Cohen, may be traveling with him.

Case Details: From the early 1970s, Myron Shapiro operated a series of businesses illegally selling pornography through the U.S. mail. On June 8, 1988, he was indicted by a federal grand jury in Pennsylvania. On January 30, 1989, he was convicted. He failed to appear in court for sentencing and later fled U.S. jurisdiction. Shapiro has visited Israel, Europe, and the Caribbean islands. The U.S. is requesting extradition from any country which has a treaty with the U.S. which permits extradition for the offenses charged.

CONSIDERED ARMED AND DANGEROUS.

WANTED
SEXUAL BATTERY OF A MINOR

FREDERICK STILES WANAMAKER

Unlawful flight to avoid prosecution – aggravated sexual battery on a minor

WANTED BY THE FBI

Photograph taken in 1995

ALIAS: Frederick Stiles

DESCRIPTION

DATE OF BIRTH USED: January 21, 1947
PLACE OF BIRTH: Nyack, New York
HEIGHT: 5'8"
WEIGHT: 180lbs
HAIR: Brown
EYES: Blue
SCARS, MARKS, TATTOOS: None known

SEX: Male
RACE: White
NATIONALITY: American
OCCUPATIONS: Wanamaker has worked as a Merchant Marine and a ship's captain. He has training and credentials which qualify him to pilot any seagoing vessel anywhere in the world.
NCIC: W971937620

REMARKS: Wanamaker's last known address was in Englewood, North Carolina. He has ties to Florida, Texas, Virginia, the Cayman Islands, Indonesia, and Nassau, Bahamas.

CAUTION

It is alleged that between 1985 and 1997, Frederick Stiles Wanamaker sexually molested five minor boys on numerous occasions in Buckingham County, Virginia. On April 11, 2000, Wanamaker was indicted by a Buckingham County Grand Jury on twenty-one counts of aggravated sexual battery and sodomy. On September 11, 2001, a federal arrest warrant was issued by the Western District of Virginia, Lynchburg, Virginia, charging Wanamaker with unlawful flight to avoid prosecution.

WANTED
FOR BANK FRAUD

TEREZINHA QUEIROZ BODOTT
REWARD

Bank Fraud; conspiracy to commit bank fraud

WANTED BY THE FBI

ALIASES: J. Terezinha DeSouza, Terezinha Queiroz-Bodott, Terezinha Queiroz, Terezinha Q. Bodott, Teresa Queiroz, Terezinha Souza, Terezinha Sosa, Teresa Sosa, Terezinha Sosa Barbanell, Theresa Q. Bodott, Teresa Dudogt, Terezinha S. Barbanell, Teresa Barbanell, Teresa Bodott, Adriana Bodott, Terezinha Quiroz, Terezinha DeSousa, Terezinha Generoso, Adriana Barbanell

DESCRIPTION

DATE OF BIRTH: August 25, 1957	**SEX:** Female
PLACE OF BIRTH: Guaraniacu, Parana, Brazil	**RACE:** White
HEIGHT: 5'5"	**NATIONALITY:** Brazilian
WEIGHT: 135lbs	**OCCUPATIONS:** Telemarketer, investment broker, freelance photographer, office worker at a car dealership
HAIR: Brown	
EYES: Brown	
SCARS, MARKS, TATTOOS: None known	**NCIC:** W170100778

REMARKS: Bodott has resided in Phoenix, Arizona; the Bronx and Queens sections of New York City; Pomona and Claremont, California; Miami Beach, Homestead, and Miami, Florida; and Plano, Texas where she operated an ostrich farm. She has also resided in Brazil and may have returned there. In addition, she has ties to Aspen, Colorado; Lawrence, Massachusetts; and the New York Metropolitan area. She claims to have a degree in Business Administration.

CAUTION

From May through July of 1999, Terezinha Queiroz Bodott allegedly accessed and conducted unauthorized withdrawals using ATM debits and electronic wire transfers of funds over $100,000 from the inactive account of a deceased couple. Bodott was assisted by an associate who was a bank officer. Bodott accessed the account from various banking facilities in the Miami and Fort Lauderdale, Florida areas. On July 2, 1999, an arrest warrant was issued for Bodott who is still at large. Her associate is currently serving time in prison.

WANTED
SWINDLING

ANN L. CORRICELLI

REWARD

WANTED BY ILLINOIS STATE POLICE

DESCRIPTION

DATE OF BIRTH: August 10, 1963	**HAIR:** Dark
HEIGHT: 5'0"	**SEX:** Female
WEIGHT: 140 lbs	**RACE:** White

THE DETAILS SURROUNDING THE CRIME

As of this writing, mother and daughter team Marie Wilson and Ann Corricelli, of East Peoria, Illinois, are still free and are probably somewhere in Europe. They are charged with swindling fifteen women out of $600,000. Additional victims are known to the police but those victims refuse to press charges or testify in court; they are too humiliated and embarrassed at being gullible. Undoubtedly there are other, unknown victims who for the same reason will not admit their involvement with the fortune tellers to the police.

One of the victims who has agreed to testify, Mrs. Josephine Wallace, a widow, was swindled out of over $200,000 in cash and jewelry. The fortune tellers also got her to buy them a $30,000 Cadillac DeVille. The second largest loser was a woman taken for $180,000. Most of the victims were elderly although there were several college-educated professional women in their twenties and thirties among the victims.

After one client complained to police about Wilson and Corricelli, bunco officers initiated an investigation which included questioning people seen visiting the Corricelli home and others who received numerous telephone calls from that house. Word of the investigation soon got back to the fortune tellers from some of those questioned and mother and daughter abruptly left town before they could be arrested. Although Marie Wilson was subsequently captured and returned to Illinois, she posted bond and again vanished. Contact David Rebman – Illinois State Police at (309) 692-2100.

WANTED
FOR FRAUD

CARL EDWARD FUERST
$10,000 REWARD

Theft or receipt of stolen mail, obstruction of correspondence, and bank fraud

WANTED BY U.S POSTAL INSPECTION SERVICE
U.S. MARSHALS SERVICE
FBI

ALIASES: Carl E. Fuerst, Shawn P. Gibson, Douglas R. Alderman, Gerald P. Cole, Johnny W. Hall, Carl Snyder, Douglas Alderman, Johnni Hall, Carl Phillips, Douglas Cole, John Doe, Shawn Gibson, Ralph Dillard, David Russell, Taylor Robinson, Dale McTaggart, Kevin Jernigan, Jimmy Crumpton, Carl Roberts, Donny Hamblin, Thomas Houston, Donald Smith, Donnie Bridgeman, David Gillentine, Ricky Hallmark, Phillip McKoy, John McCillum, Thomas May, James Barnes, Bill Perry, Phillip Poteet, Shawn R. Gibson, Douglas R. Alderman, Shannon Shurholt, Leach Howard, Brad Waycaster, Bill Berry, Johnny Hall, Ronnie Foster.

DESCRIPTION

DATES OF BIRTH USED: September 7, 1966, August 30, 1954	**HAIR:** Brown
PLACE OF BIRTH: Torrence, CA	**EYES:** Brown or blue
HEIGHT: 5'9"	**SEX:** Male
WEIGHT: 190 lbs	**RACE:** White
	NCIC: W070190808

CAR USED: May be driving a dark blue or green newer model Chevy Lumina (with spoiler), Possibly a Ford Fairmont or Plymouth Fury type vehicle - late 80's or early 90's model, light in color, possibly a little darker color on top and possibly a (2) two door and a darker colored Toyota Camry.

CAUTION

Fuerst has been identified as the person responsible for burglaries to post office boxes, forgeries and bank fraud in at least 17 states in the south and midwest regions of the United States. Fuerst's criminal activity dates back to 1996 and he has numerous outstanding felony warrants. Fuerst is currently being sought by the United States Marshals Service, the United States Postal service, and numerous state, county, and local law enforcement agencies.

CONSIDERED ARMED AND DANGEROUS.
DO NOT ATTEMPT TO APPREHEND THIS PERSON YOURSELF.

CRIME ALERT
CARL EDWARD FUERST

Carl Edward Fuerst is wanted by U.S. Postal Inspectors for Theft or Receipt of Stolen Mail, Obstruction of Correspon-dence and Bank Fraud. His prior arrests includes Passing Worthless Checks, False Identification, Aiding and Abetting, Probation Violation, Passing Counterfeit Currency, Fugitive From Justice, Transporting, Delivering or Possession of Counterfeit Currency, Armed and Dangerous, Attempted Escape, Larceny, Mail Theft, Theft of Government Property, Bank Fraud, Passing Forged Instrument, Fraud, Forgery, Theft, Attempted Escape and False Identification. The suspect is a multi-state offender with prior arrests in Nevada, California, Virginia, Louisiana, North Carolina, Texas, Colorado, Georgia, Missouri, Oklahoma, Indiana, Arizona and Mississippi. His arrest record dates back to June 1988. Carl Edward Fuerst is wanted in sixteen states for Breaking and Entering Post Office Boxes, Stealing Checks, Washing Checks and Counterfeiting. He currently, as of December 29, 2001, has active warrants for his arrest. Carl Edward Fuerst is considered to be an escape risk and a white supremacist. Fuerst may be staying at hotels/motels along the interstates or with other white supremacists or Christian Identity groups may be housing him. His last known activities were in Tennessee in December 2001. He is always clean-shaven and neat in appearance. On cooler days he is known to wear a dark leather jacket or sweater. He wears a watch and a wedding band. He has been known to frequent Wal-Mart Stores. All Law Enforcement should use caution when trying to identify this individual, as he has been known to use stolen or false identifications in the past. He should be considered armed and dangerous, as he has previously brandished a weapon when confronted. He has been seen with a .22 and has been known to purchase 9mm ammunition.

WANTED
FOR BANK FRAUD

JOHN RUFFO
REWARD

Violating conditions of release

WANTED BY U.S. MARSHALS

DESCRIPTION

DATE OF BIRTH USED: November 26, 1954	**EYES:** Brown
PLACE OF BIRTH: New York	**SEX:** Male
HEIGHT: 5'5"	**RACE:** White
WEIGHT: 170 lbs	**SCARS, MARKS:** None
HAIR: Brown	**NCIC #:** W11611894

CAUTION

Ruffo failed to surrender as scheduled at a federal prison in New Jersey, where he was to serve 17 years on more than 150 counts of bank fraud, money laundering, wire fraud and conspiracy. He defrauded several banks of $350 million
 DO NOT ATTEMPT TO APPREHEND THIS PERSON YOURSELF. If you have any information concerning John Ruffo, you should contact the nearest US MARSHALS OFFICE, U.S. embassy or consulate. Or call the U.S. Marshals Service at 1-800-336-0102. The identities of individuals who furnish information will be kept in strict confidence. The U.S. will pay an appropriate reward for information that leads to the arrest of John Ruffo.

INTERNATIONAL CRIME ALERT
JOHN RUFFO

CASE DETAILS: John Ruffo and his associate, Edward (Ed) J. Reiners, developed an elaborate scheme which defrauded more than ten banks of $350 million dollars. Reiners, a former employee of Phillip Morris, went to several banks and pretended that he was in charge of a "top-secret" project for the tobacco company. Ruffo introduced himself as being in charge of purchasing computers for this phantom project. Reiners and Ruffo used the money that they borrowed from the banks to invest in the stock market. According to investigators, both lost miserably in the market.

Over the course of two years, the "project" that Ruffo and Reiners thought up kept growing and growing. Nine US and international banks were on-board. The con men met with Vice Presidents from these banks, convincing them to hand over hundreds of millions of dollars to the bogus operation. The plan unraveled when an official from the Long Term Credit Bank of Japan called Phillip Morris and asked for Reiners. He was shocked to hear that Reiners hadn't worked there in almost three years.

The con men were arrested and convicted. Reiners is currently serving a 16 and a half year sentence.

In March 1996, John Ruffo was convicted of one-hundred sixty counts of bank fraud, money laundering, wire fraud and conspiracy. He cost several foreign and U.S. banks more than three-hundred fifty

million dollars. Ruffo pleaded guilty and was sentenced to seventeen years in prison. Ruffo was released on ten-million dollars bail. On November 9th, 1998, authorities ordered him to report to prison in Fairton, New Jersey. Ruffo never did. Later that day, Ruffo's rental car was found at JFK airport. Authorities believe John Ruffo had escaped American jurisdiction.

The U.S. Marshals Service has asked the Federal Deposit Insurance Corporation (FDIC) to alert all U.S. banks about the current activities of fugitive John Ruffo, who was convicted in 1998 for his role in defrauding several banks of over $350 million and may now be attempting another fraud scheme.

Mr. Ruffo was recently seen in several banks in Duncan, Oklahoma, trying to arrange large wire transfers. In each instance, he asked to see the bank president and stated he wanted to set up an account to receive wire transfers of large sums of money from Nigeria. He said that he is employed as a liquidator and earns his money from finder's fees. He used his real name, John Ruffo, but he may also attempt to use an alias.

Mr. Ruffo has been a federal fugitive since he failed to report to prison in 1998 to serve a 17-year sentence for bank fraud. The fraudulent business scheme involved phony equipment leases and an individual posing as an official of the Philip Morris Company.

The U.S. Marshals Service has asked that anyone who sees Mr. Ruffo or has information about him to immediately call the local police.

WANTED
FRAUD

GONZALO ANTHONY QUINONES

Fraud by wire; mail fraud

WANTED BY THE FBI

Photograph taken in 1995

ALIASES: Anthony Gonzalo Quinones, Tony Quinones, Anthony G. Quinones, Anthony Quinones-Ulloa, Anthony G. Ulloa, Anthony Q. Ulloa, Antonio Gonzalo Ulloa, Antonio Gonzalo Quinones, Arthur Braccio, Tony Arena

DESCRIPTION

DATE OF BIRTH USED: November 3, 1965
PLACE OF BIRTH: Costa Rica
HEIGHT: 5'11"
WEIGHT: 175 to 200 pounds
HAIR: Brown
EYES: Brown/Hazel

SCARS, MARKS, TATTOOS: Quinones has a tattoo of a scorpion on his left shoulder.
SEX: Male
RACE: White (Hispanic)
NATIONALITY: Costa Rican
OCCUPATIONS: Computer company owner
NCIC: W961114146

REMARKS: Quinones has ties to Jacksonville, Florida; Lynn, Massachusetts; Boston, Massachusetts; and Costa Rica.

CAUTION

Gonzalo Anthony Quinones owned and operated a computer business located in Seminole, Florida, from March of 1999 to October of 1999. The business was custom built computers which were sold on an Internet auction site. A review of the business' financial records revealed that Quinones had allegedly misused funds for his personal use. It was also revealed that over 250 customers never received their computers after paying for them.

On October 23, 2000, a federal arrest warrant was issued for Quinones in the Middle District of Florida charging him with fraud by wire and mail fraud.

Quinones is also wanted by the Pinellas County Sheriff's Office, Largo, Florida, on charges of failure to appear and a lewd and lascivious act on a minor.

WANTED

FOR MAIL FRAUD

HENRY ELDON STRICKER & KAREN LYNN STRICKER

REWARD

WANTED BY THE U.S. POSTAL SERVICE

Henry Eldon Stricker

Karen Lynn Stricker

DESCRIPTIONS

DATE OF BIRTH February 25, 1959	DATE OF BIRTH December 26, 1957
HEIGHT 6'2"	HEIGHT 5'10"
WEIGHT 180 lbs	WEIGHT 225 lbs
HAIR Blonde/Brown	HAIR Brown
EYES Blue	EYES Blue
SEX Male	SEX Female
RACE White	RACE White
OCCUPATION Real estate agent, salesman	OCCUPATION Interior decorator
NCIC # W821576770	NCIC # W822090537

CAUTION

From 1983 through 1989, Henry Stricker and his wife Karen operated out of Los Angeles, California, perpetrating nationwide fraud. Numerous victims were induced to buy outlets to sell merchandise display racks. But the purchasers never received the promised outlets and were defrauded of more than five million dollars.

On December 3, 1992, the Strickers were indicted by a federal grand jury on thirty counts of mail fraud, wire fraud, interstate transportation of stolen property, false statements to a government agency and obstruction of justice. Both of the accused failed to appear for trial and subsequently fled the U.S. If convicted on all accounts, Henry Stricker could receive two-hundred fifteen years and a fine of eight and a half million dollars. Karen Stricker could receive one-hundred ninety-five years in prison and a fine of seven and a half million dollars.

If you have any information concerning Henry Eldon Stricker and Karen Lynn Stricker, you should contact the U.S. Postal Inspection Service at 1-800-654-8896, or the nearest U.S. embassy or consulate. The U.S. guarantees that all reports will be investigated and all information will be kept confidential. If appropriate, the U.S. is prepared to protect informants by relocating them.

WANTED
FOR BANK FRAUD

GANIYU SAMUEL SOUNGA

Fraud and related activity in connection with identification documents and information; fraud and related activity in connection with access devices, and bank fraud.

REWARD

WANTED BY U.S POSTAL SERVICE

ALIASES: Ganiyu Sonuga; Ganlyu S. Sonuga; Ganiyu Sam Sonuga; and Monsurat Sounga.

DESCRIPTION

DATE OF BIRTH: July 26, 1956	**EYES:** Brown
PLACE BIRTH: Nigeria	**SEX:** Male
HEIGHT: 6'0"	**RACE:** White
WEIGHT: 185lbs	**OCCUPATION:** Cab driver, delivery person
HAIR: Bald	**NCIC #:** W261291730

VIOLATION: Title 18 USC 1028: Fraud and related activity in connection with identification documents and information; Title 18 USC 1029: Fraud and related activity in connection with access devices; and Title 18 USC 1344: Bank fraud. U.S. Postal Inspectors' 24-hour phone: (800) 300-3492 Outside the U.S.: (617) 654-5916 Northeast Division, Boston, MA, or Postal Crime Hotline at (800) 654-8896.

WANTED

FOR WIRE FRAUD

VIRGINIA LO YAO

REWARD

WANTED BY U.S POSTAL INSPECTION

ALIASES: Virginia L Loyao, Virginia,L Yoa, Virginia,L Yao, Gina Yao

DESCRIPTION

DATE OF BIRTH: September 9, 1963	**EYES:** Brown
PLACE BIRTH: Philippines	**SEX:** Female
HEIGHT: 5'1"	**RACE:** Philippine
WEIGHT: 120 lbs	**OCCUPATIONS:** Office manager
HAIR: Brown	**NCIC #:** W16611286

CAUTION

The last known residence for Virginia Lo Yao was Los Angeles, CA. Anyone with information on the whereabouts of fugitive Virginia Lo Yao should call IFRS Group at 714-562-0882. Callers may remain anonymous if desired.

DO NOT ATTEMPT TO APPREHEND THIS PERSON YOURSELF. SHE SHOULD BE CONSIDERED ARMED AND DANGEROUS. REPORT ANY INFORMATION TO 714-562-0882

WANTED
FOR WIRE FRAUD

MICHAEL WALDO ZWICKEL

REWARD

WANTED BY THE FBI

ALIASES: Michael Zwickel, Mike Zwickel, Harry L. Flackman, Harry Flackman

DESCRIPTION

DATE OF BIRTH:	April 29, 1950	SEX: Male
PLACE BIRTH:	South Dakota	RACE: White
HEIGHT:	5'10"	OCCUPATIONS: Title company owner and operator,
WEIGHT:	220 lbs	EKG technician, cardiac catherization technician,
HAIR:	Blonde/Brown	lawyer, musician
EYES:	Hazel/Brown	NCIC #: W280443326

CAUTION

It is alleged that between December of 1995 and December of 1996, Michael Waldo Zwickel defrauded various lending institutions out of money and property in New Jersey, California, Indiana, and Illinois. After learning he was under investigation, Zwickel left suicide notes for his wife and children on December 30, 1996, and disappeared. His whereabouts since are unknown. On January 19, 2000, a six count indictment was returned against Michael Waldo Zwickel by a Federal Grand Jury in the Southern District of Indiana, Indianapolis, Indiana, charging him with wire fraud. A federal arrest warrant was then issued for Zwickel on January 20, 2000. He has had medical training and is a disbarred lawyer.

WANTED
ARSON

GEORGE ANTHONY ORFANOS

REWARD

WANTED BY BUREAU OF ALCOHOL, TOBACCO AND FIREARMS

DESCRIPTION

DATE OF BIRTH: July 20, 1949	**SEX:** Male
PLACE OF BIRTH: Athens, Greece	**RACE:** White
HEIGHT: 6'1"	**SCARS/TATTOOS:** None visible
WEIGHT: 200 lbs	**OCCUPATION:** Painting contractor
HAIR: Black	**NCIC #:** W160516101 (CR98-508)
EYES: Brown	

CAUTION

Orfanos is wanted for setting a fire which destroyed a $4.5 million mansion in Sacramento, CA. He is known to have lived in the Atlanta, GA area as well as in Sacramento, CA. Orfanos has a pronounced Greek accent and speaks "broken English." A Federal Arrest Warrant (92-312JFM) was issued for Orfanos on December 17, 1992 in the Eastern Judicial District, Sacramento, California. The warrant charges Orfanos with Conspiracy (18 USC 371), Arson (18 USC 844(i)), Arson to Commit Felony (18 USC 844(h)(1)), Mail Fraud (18 USC 1341), and Interstate Transportation of Fraudulently Obtained Property (18 USC 2314).

WANTED
ARSON

INFORMATION NEEDED
$1,000 REWARD

Riverside, CA: On March 18, 2001 at 6:49 pm, an Arson Fire was set in the industrial warehouse building, located at 12105 Madera Way in Riverside, California. Investigators ruled that an arsonist intentionally set this fire, which caused at least a half a million dollars in damage. It was also determined by investigators that a flammable liquid was used in the setting of the fire. The Riverside Fire Department's Arson Investigation Unit is seeking the help of anyone who may have information about the arsonist, the vehicle used, or any other information that may give investigators the clue they need to break the case. Call We Tip Arson Hotline at 800-47-ARSON.

WANTED
ARSON

INFORMATION NEEDED
$5,000 REWARD

Arson Investigators are asking for the public's help in apprehending the suspect(s) responsible for a recent fire which occurred in Redwood Estates, in Santa Clara County, California. On August 14, 2000 at approximately 12:30 a.m., unknown suspect(s) carried a large wood and cardboard shipping box (used to ship a utility trailer) from the yard of one residence on Mary Alice Drive to a small outside building located at the residence of 18020 Madrone Drive. The Building was occupied, with the window open and the TV on. At approximately 12:40 a.m., the resident inside the building at 18020 Madrone heard noises outside, so he turned off the TV and looked outside but saw nothing, and the noises stopped. At approximately 1:10 the box was placed under the window and next to the only door leading out of the building. The box was lit on fire and quickly started burning the outside of the building. The occupant, who had fallen asleep, awoke to the window breaking from the heat of the fire. The side and roof of the building was on fire. The occupant was able to escape uninjured. Investigators believe that there was more than one suspect involved in this Arson fire. Call We Tip Arson Hotline at 800-47-ARSON.

WANTED
FOR BANK ROBBERY

NOVA ESTHER GUTHRIE
$50,000 REWARD
WANTED BY THE FBI

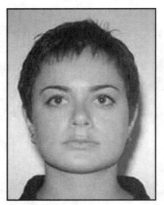
Photograph taken in 1999

Photograph taken in 1997

Photograph taken in 1998

ALIASES: Nova Hicks, Nova Thomas, Alex Santini

DESCRIPTION

DATE OF BIRTH: June 6, 1973
PLACE OF BIRTH: Colorado
HEIGHT: 5'4"
WEIGHT: 130 lbs
NCIC: W156016411
OCCUPATION: Waitress

SCARS, MARKS, TATTOOS: Tattoos on her back and left hip. She also has a pierced abdomen.
HAIR: Brown
EYES: Brown
SEX: Female
RACE: Caucasian
NATIONALITY: American

REMARKS: Nova Guthrie is an avid snowboarder and likes to frequent ski resorts. Guthrie is believed to be traveling with an alleged accomplice, Craig Michael Pritchert.

CAUTION
Nova Esther Guthrie and Craig Michael Pritchert are wanted for allegedly robbing numerous banks throughout the Pacific Northwest, Texas, Arizona, New Mexico, and Colorado, dating back to 1997. In advance of a robbery, Pritchert and Guthrie are believed to spend considerable time in the area in order to study and surveil the targeted bank. Each robbery is an armed take-over of the bank, and often occurs around the time the bank opens or closes. Pritchert and Guthrie, sometimes accompanied by another male, generally are able to access money from the bank's vault, and often tie up their victims prior to leaving the bank. They wear disguises during a robbery and maintain radio contact with their co-conspirator(s) on the outside via two-way radios. They usually abandon their getaway vehicle not far from the bank.
SHOULD BE CONSIDERED ARMED AND DANGEROUS

WANTED
FOR BANK ROBBERY

CRAIG MICHAEL PRITCHERT
$50,000 REWARD
WANTED BY THE FBI

Photograph taken in 1998 Photograph taken in 1998 Photograph taken in 1998

ALIASES: Josh Riggs, Wil Hicks, Garrett W. Guthrite, John Guthrite, Brent Wilson Hicks, Matthew Ryan Pritchat, Michael Craig Pritchart, Craig Pritchart

DESCRIPTION

DATES OF BIRTH USED: February 1, 1963; February 13, 1963; February 5, 1965; February 13, 1961; August 9, 1962
PLACE OF BIRTH: Illinois
HEIGHT: 6'0"
WEIGHT: 185 lbs
NCIC: W040057174

OCCUPATION: Day Trader on the Internet
SCARS, MARKS, TATTOOS: Pritchert has a scar on his abdomen.
HAIR: Light brown
EYES: Blue
SEX: Male
RACE: White
NATIONALITY: American

REMARKS: Craig Michael Pritchert is an avid snowboarder and likes to frequent ski resorts and health clubs. Pritchert is believed to be traveling with an alleged accomplice, Nova Esther Guthrie.

CAUTION

Craig Michael Pritchert and Nova Esther Guthrie are wanted for allegedly robbing numerous banks throughout the Pacific Northwest, Texas, Arizona, New Mexico, and Colorado, dating back to 1997. In advance of a robbery, Pritchert and Guthrie are believed to spend considerable time in the area in order to study and surveil the targeted bank. Each robbery is an armed take-over of the bank, and often occurs around the time the bank opens or closes. Pritchert and Guthrie, sometimes accompanied by another male, generally are able to access money from the bank's vault, and often tie up their victims prior to leaving the bank. They wear disguises during a robbery and maintain radio contact with their co-conspirator(s) on the outside via two-way radios. They usually abandon their getaway vehicle not far from the bank.

SHOULD BE CONSIDERED ARMED AND DANGEROUS

WANTED
BANK ROBBERY, RACKETEERING

SALVATORE DEMEO

REWARD

Racketeering; racketeering conspiracy; bank robbery; bank robbery conspiracy,
Hobbs act – armored car robbery

WANTED BY THE FBI

ALIASES: "Sal", "Sallie"

DESCRIPTION

DATES OF BIRTH USED: January 4, 1940, January 4, 1939	**EYES:** Brown
PLACE OF BIRTH: New York	**SEX:** Male
HEIGHT: 5'10"	**RACE:** White
WEIGHT: 190 lbs	**NATIONALITY:** American
HAIR: Gray	**SCARS/TATTOOS:** Scar upper left arm, left hand
	NCIC #: W962477506

REMARKS: : Demeo slumps over when he walks and enjoys playing golf

CAUTION

Salvatore Demeo is an alleged member of a large organized crime family based in New York City. He has been implicated in a series of crimes including the August 29, 1996, armed robbery of a bank in Manalapan, New Jersey, in which approximately $400,000 was stolen. He is also wanted for conspiring to rob a Brinks armored car in the Fall of 1996 in New York City. Additionally, Demeo is wanted for allegedly conspiring to rob another armored car in 1997 and the same bank in New Jersey in 1998. He was indicted for these crimes in the Eastern District of New York on April 25, 2001.

SHOULD BE CONSIDERED ARMED AND DANGEROUS.

WANTED
FOR ARMED ROBBERY

FILIBERTO OJEDA RIOS
$500,000 REWARD

Aggravated robbery of federally insured bank funds, conspiracy to interfere with commerce by robbery; foreign and interstate transportation of stolen money – bond default

WANTED BY THE FBI

ALIASES: F. Salas Arias, Efrain Centeno, Juvenal Concepcion Cruzado, Alberto Dominguez, Andres Gonzalez, Juan Leon, Jose Mario, J. Marrero, Felipe Ortega, Julio Lopez Pabon, Francisco Pastrana, J. Perez, Rafael Perez, Pedro Rosario Ramirez, Pedro Ramos, J. Rodriguez, Luis Rodriguez, Pedro Rosario, Torres, Pedro Almodovar Rivera

DESCRIPTION

DATES OF BIRTH USED: April 23, 1933, April 28. 1930
PLACE OF BIRTH: Naguabo, Puerto Rico
HEIGHT: 5'8"
WEIGHT: 150 to 170 pounds
OCCUPATION: Musician (trumpet and guitar)
HAIR: Gray
EYES: Brown

SCARS AND MARKS: Ojeda Rios has a scar on his chest from heart surgery, uses a pacemaker, and walks with a slight limp.
SEX: Male
RACE: White
NATIONALITY: American
NCIC #: W604921641

REMARKS: Ojeda Rios wears prescription glasses, normally wears a beard, and may have his hair dyed black. He is believed to be living with his wife in the mountainous region of central Puerto Rico and may travel to the Continental United States. He is known to possess automatic weapons and explosives, and in the past, has fired upon law enforcement officials.

CAUTION

Filiberto Ojeda Rios is the leader of the "Ejercito Popular Boricua (Puerto Rican Army of the People) - Los Macheteros." Based in Puerto Rico, this clandestine terrorist group has claimed responsibility for numerous armed robberies and terrorist bombings since 1978. Ojeda Rios is being sought in connection with the September 12, 1983, armed robbery of $7.2 million from the Wells Fargo Depot in Hartford, Connecticut. He is also wanted for bond default in September of 1990. In July of 1992, Filiberto Ojeda Rios was sentenced in absentia to 55 years in prison and fined $600,000.

WANTED
MONEY LAUNDERING

JOSE ALVAREZ TOSTADO

REWARD

Conspiracy to launder monetary instruments, laundering of monetary instruments, continuing criminal enterprise

WANTED BY U.S. CUSTOMS

ALIASES: El Compadre, Compadre Ford, Jose Gonzales

DESCRIPTION

DATE OF BIRTH USED: August 27, 1955	**EYES:** Blue
PLACE OF BIRTH: Mexico	**SEX:** Male
HEIGHT: 5'10"	**RACE:** White
WEIGHT: 280 lbs	**SCARS/TATTOOS:** None visible
HAIR: Brown (balding)	**NCIC #:** W160516101 (CR98-508)

CAUTION

As part of Operation Casablanca, ALVAREZ was indicted in May 1998, in the Central District of California, for money laundering, conspiracy to distribute narcotics and being a principal member of a continuing criminal enterprise. Attempts to locate ALVAREZ has proved futile. In February 1999, information was received which indicates that ALVAREZ may be in Bogota, Colombia, and remains a U.S. Customs Fugitive.

WANTED

FORGERY

CHARLES MATHIS

$1,000 REWARD

Forgery and theft by deception

WANTED BY PENNSYLVANIA STATE POLICE

DESCRIPTION

AGE: 60	**SEX:** Male
HEIGHT: 5'8"	**RACE:** Black
WEIGHT: 201 lbs	**DISTINGUISHING CHARACTERISTICS:** Pointed
HAIR: Bald	"Spock-Like" Ears
EYES: Brown	

CAUTION

The Pennsylvania state police, Butler County, is seeking the whereabouts of Charles Edward Mathis for forgery and theft by deception. On the evening of November 8, 1999, Mathis arrived at a Giant Eagle grocery store in Center Township, Butler County, Pennsylvania. He presented what appeared to be an employee check from Bob Evans restaurant to a teller and received cash in the amount of $395.00 The check was written on a false account and investigators have learned that the check was counterfeit. Identical checks have been passed in Washington, Allegheny, Crawford and York counties. The subject has identification cards in the states of Tennessee, Ohio and West Virginia; it is assumed that similar transactions have occurred in these states. Addresses listed by Mathis in Knoxville, Tennessee, and at 147 Ohio Street, Washington, Pennsylvania have proven to be false. Authorities have issued a warrant for the suspect. The warrant was issued under the assumed name of Charles Edward Mathis; it is unknown what the suspect's actual name may be. Call 1-800-4PA TIPS with any information.

WANTED
FIREARMS SMUGGLING

ROBERT MA

REWARD

WANTED BY U.S. CUSTOMS

ALIASES: Bao Ping Ma, Robert Ping Chung Ma

DESCRIPTION

DATE OF BIRTH: March 28, 1952	**EYES:** Brown
PLACE OF BIRTH: China	**SEX:** Male
HEIGHT: 5'8"	**RACE:** Asian
WEIGHT: 145 lbs	**SCARS, MARKS, TATTOOS:** None visible
HAIR: Black	**WARRANT #:** 3-96-30152-OEW

CAUTION

On June 4, 1996, Robert MA aka Bao Ping MA or Robert Ping Chung MA, was indicted by a Federal Grand Jury in the northern district of California for smuggling firearms in violation of Title 18 United States Code Sections 545 and 922. MA was indicted along with 13 other individuals for various weapons and money laundering violations. MA is believed to and should be considered Armed and Dangerous. It's alleged that MA participated in the unlawful smuggling into the U.S. of 20,000 rifle bipods using a People's Republic of China company. It's alleged MA participated in the smuggling of 2000 fully automatic machine guns from another People's Republic of China company. It is also alleged MA participated in the distribution of machine gun silencers manufactured in China for entry into the U.S. MA travels to China regularly, however, he was last seen in the San Francisco, California area.

WANTED
FOR ESCAPE

RAYMOND TUDOR
REWARD

A Canada-wide warrant has been issued for Tudor's arrest on a charge of
Escape from Lawful Custody

WANTED BY THE ROYAL CANADIAN
MOUNTED POLICE

DESCRIPTION

DATE OF BIRTH:	August 29, 1953	**EYES:**	Blue
HEIGHT:	5'10"	**SEX:**	Male
WEIGHT:	225 lbs	**RACE:**	White
HAIR:	Brown		

CAUTION

The RCMP is assisting Corrections Service Canada in locating Raymond John Tudor. Tudor, formerly of Calgary, Alberta, suffers from Parkinson's Disease, a disease of the central nervous system which causes shaking, tremors and weakness. Tudor's hair is described as long and when last seen wore a long beard that was starting to grey. Tudor wears prescription lenses. Tudor was serving two life sentences without chance of parole for 20 years as a result of two convictions for Second Degree Murder.

WANTED

FOR VIOLATION OF PROBATION

JOHN VINCENT VU

REWARD

WANTED U.S MARSHALS

DESCRIPTION

DATE OF BIRTH: August 23, 1976	EYES: Brown
PLACE OF BIRTH: Pennsylvania	SEX: Male
HEIGHT: 6'0"	RACE: Asian
WEIGHT: 150 lbs	SCARS/TATTOOS: Scar upper left arm, left hand
HAIR: Brown	NCIC #: W962477506

CAUTION

Vu has been charged with violating federal probation for his original charges of bank fraud. He has also been charged with first degree murder by the Chicago Police Department for participating in a gang shooting. Vu is Vietnamese and a known member of the Asian gang, GAP Family Street Gang.

SHOULD BE CONSIDERED ARMED AND DANGEROUS.
DO NOT ATTEMPT TO APPREHEND THIS PERSON YOURSELF.

WANTED
TRANSPORT OF STOLEN GOODS

LUAR VETUS LORRET

International transportation of stolen goods

WANTED BY U.S. CUSTOMS

ALIAS: Demis V. Astor

DESCRIPTION

DATE OF BIRTH: February 13, 1957	**EYES:** Green
PLACE OF BIRTH: Balkash, Lithuania, Russia	**SEX:** Male
HEIGHT: 5'11"	**RACE:** White
WEIGHT: 190 lbs	**SCARS/TATTOOS:** None
HAIR: Brown	**WARRANT #:** 97-9092-CR-RYSKAMP

CAUTION

In July 1997, LORRET was indicted in the Southern District of Florida for nine counts for transportation of stolen goods. LORRET organized a scheme to defraud the Republic of Tatarstan of nine shipments of oil valued at 6.3 million dollars. LORRET was the mastermind and organized his scheme by telling various Russian government representatives that he was experienced in the sale of oil products world wide and had contacts that could sell Tatarstan's products to obtain United States currency for the Tartars. AVTNPO Kazan, the Kazan Foreign Trade, Scientific and Industrial Association, (a quasi-government agency of the Republic of Tatartstan), which is responsible for finding customers to purchase Tatarstan products, authorized the oil shipments based on the scheme LORRET had created. A Russian representative traveled to the United States seeking to obtain payment for the oil from LORRET. LORRET first attempted to bribe the representative. But when the bribe failed, LORRET brandished weapons and threatened the representative with bodily harm. LORRET is a Russian national. He is believed to reside in the Los Angeles, California, or Las Vegas, Nevada, area. LORRET speaks English, and falsely brags that he served with the Russian Army and was on the Russian Olympic shooting team. He should be considered armed and dangerous. LORRET is a U.S. Customs fugitive.

CONSIDERED ARMED AND DANGEROUS.

WANTED
FOR COUNTERFEITING

JAMES GUILLET

WANTED BY THE ROYAL CANADIAN MOUNTED POLICE

ALIASES: James Guillet, Cory Lee McLeod, James Edward Joseph McQuaid, Roberto Bandiera

DESCRIPTION

HEIGHT: 6 feet	**SEX:** Male
WEIGHT: 219 pounds	**RACE:** Black
HAIR: Black	**SCARS/TATTOOS:** Vertical scars on face
EYES: Black	**RCMP FILE #:** 99-MEFI-3644

CAUTION

Details: Subject deals in the counterfeiting of various official government documents such as Canadian passports, driver's licenses and citizenship cards. The subject's real identity is unknown. The documents which are counterfeited can be sold for significant profit and can assist other criminals in other activities, i.e. importation of drugs and illegally obtaining Canadian citizenship. The subject has an outstanding arrest warrant issued in the name of James Guillet out of the RCMP's Kingston detachment and is the main suspect in a passport investigation out of Montreal.

WANTED
FOR FRAUD

LI ZHOU

Mailing threatening or extortionate interstate communications; threatening to tamper with consumer products

WANTED BY THE FBI

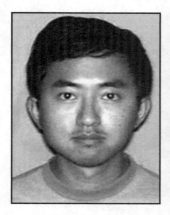 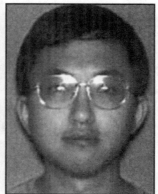

ALIASES: David Hong, Grant C. Yang, Edward Y. Lee, Zhou Li

DESCRIPTION

DATES OF BIRTH USED: March 11, 1973; September 18, 1976; November 21, 1979; April 25, 1976	**SCARS, MARKS, TATTOOS:** Zhou has two moles on his left cheek.
PLACE OF BIRTH: China	**SEX:** Male
HEIGHT: 5'8"	**RACE:** Asian
WEIGHT: 145lbs	**NATIONALITY:** Chinese
HAIR: Black	**OCCUPATIONS:** Unknown
EYES: Brown	**NCIC:** W891038378

REMARKS: Zhou is believed to enjoy large college or university environments and may be enrolled as a student under an alias name. He is very proficient with computers and Internet operations, and often carries a laptop computer. He sometimes wears glasses.

CAUTION

Li Zhou is being sought for his alleged role in an attempted extortion plot. In August of 2000, it is alleged that Zhou sent letters to a large Ohio based corporation, demanding that a large sum of money be deposited into a specific Internet bank account. If his demands were not met, Zhou allegedly threatened actions which would result in a severe economic loss to the victim company. On October 6, 2000, an arrest warrant was issued in the Southern District of Ohio, Cincinnati, Ohio, charging Zhou with mailing threatening or extortionate interstate communications and threatening to tamper with consumer products. Zhou is also suspected of using stolen identities to, among other things, obtain credit cards, open bank accounts, rent apartments, and obtain official state identifications.

WANTED
ARMED BANK ROBBERY

✳ UNIDENTIFIED SUSPECT ✳
$10,000 REWARD
WANTED BY THE FBI

DESCRIPTION

ESTIMATED AGE:	Mid 30's	**HAIR:**	Black
HEIGHT:	5'10" to 6'0"	**SEX:**	Male
WEIGHT:	180 to 190 lbs	**RACE:**	White

CLOTHING: Light cargo pants and a brightly colored Hawaiian shirt, straw panama hat and dark sunglasses. The suspect was also carrying a dark green portfolio, 8½" x 11" day planner and a cell phone.

CAUTION

Washington Mutual is requesting the assistance of the public in identifying the suspect believed to be responsible for two Recent Armed Bank Robberies in South Florida. On January 10, 2000 The Branch in Ft Lauderdale at the Downtown Financial Ctr, and on January 15, 2000 in Miami at the South Dixie Hwy Branch.

WANTED
ARMED BANK ROBBERY

✳✳ UNIDENTIFIED SUSPECT ✳✳
$5,000 REWARD
WANTED BY THE FBI

The "Denim Bandit"

DESCRIPTION

ESTIMATED AGE: 28-35	**HAIR:** Brown
HEIGHT: 5'8" to 5'10"	**EYES:** Unknown
WEIGHT: 180 to 190 lbs	**SEX:** Male
BUILD: Heavy	**RACE:** White

CLOTHING: Navy Blue BB/Cap; denim shirt; blue denim pants; dark brown sunglasses; carried with a zipper top

INCIDENT DATE/TIME: Thursday, July 12, 2001/3:30 PM – Thursday, July 12, 2001/4:10 PM
LOCATION 1 : Washington Mutual Branches, 3600 Bristol St, Santa Ana, California
LOCATION 2: 12141 Garden Grove Blvd, Garden Grove, California
WEAPON: Note used, handgun threatened.

CAUTION

SUMMARY: In both robberies robber approaches teller with a black day planner type portfolio with a demand note inside which read, "This is a holdup, give me all your money, don't give me the dye pack, I have a gun." The tellers complied with the robber's wishes and gave him money from their teller drawers. No vehicle observed.

WANTED
ARMED BANK ROBBERY

∗∗ UNIDENTIFIED SUSPECT ∗∗
$10,000 REWARD

The FBI is requesting the assistance of the public in identifying the suspect pictured below. This individual is believed to be responsible for at least 10 Armed Bank Robberies in The State of California.

WANTED BY THE FBI

The "Easy Rider Bandit"

DESCRIPTION

ESTIMATED AGE:	Early 30's	HAIR:	Dark
HEIGHT:	5'10"	EYES:	Dark
WEIGHT:	160 to 170 lbs	SEX:	Male
BUILD:	Medium	RACE:	White Hispanic or Middle Eastern

CAUTION

On February 22, 2001, this suspect entered bank carrying a blue bank bag with a demand note on the top of the bag. The robber placed the bag and the note on the counter. The demand note appeared to be computer generated. The note stated, "I need $10,000. No marked bills, no dye, be calm, no jokes." No vehicle was seen. This robber is believed to be responsible for ten bank robberies in San Diego, San Bernardino, and Riverside Counties since June of 2000. He displayed a weapon during a robbery on February 23, 2001 at San Marcos, CA. Call We Tip Hotline at 1-800-78-CRIME or the FBI.

WANTED
ARMED BANK ROBBERY

** UNIDENTIFIED SUSPECT **

REWARD

WANTED BY THE CITY OF CORONA, CALIFORNIA POLICE DEPARTMENT

DESCRIPTION

ESTIMATED AGE:	17-19 / 18-20	**HAIR:**	Dark
HEIGHT:	Unknown	**EYES:**	Dark
WEIGHT:	180 to 190 lbs	**SEX:**	Male
BUILD:	Heavy	**RACE:**	Black

CLOTHING: Suspect #1: Dark pants, dark sweatshirt, back pack, light colored baseball cap, white gloves
Suspect #2: dark pants, dark jacket, back pack, white gloves

INCIDENT DATE/TIME: October 28, 2000, 9:17 am
LOCATION: 211 P.C. Bank Robbery -- PFF Bank, 410 N. McKinley, Corona
WEAPON: Black semi-automatic handgun.

CAUTION

The suspects enter a store and pull down stockings over faces. They demand money, including the safe, in a takeover robbery. Suspects were possibly in a small white American four-door vehicle. Call WeTip Hotline at 1-800-78-CRIME or the FBI.

WANTED
BANK ROBBERY

** UNIDENTIFIED SUSPECT **
$1,000 REWARD
WANTED BY THE FBI

DESCRIPTION

ESTIMATED AGE:	Early 20's	**HAIR:**	Dark
HEIGHT:	5'6" to 5'7"	**EYES:**	Dark
WEIGHT:	150 to 160 lbs	**SEX:**	Male
		RACE:	Black

CAUTION

The bank robbery suspect approaches the teller with a demand note on a napkin, the suspect makes verbal demands for "All the money" and hurries the teller. The suspect claims to be carrying a weapon but the weapon was not seen. The suspect in this case is described as follows: African American male, 5' 6" to 5' 7" tall, 150 to 160 lbs., in his early 20's. Call We Tip Hotline at 1-800-78-CRIME or the FBI.

WANTED
BANK ROBBERY

✱✱ UNIDENTIFIED SUSPECT ✱✱

$5,000 REWARD

WANTED BY THE FBI

DESCRIPTION

ESTIMATED AGE:	22-28	HAIR:	Black
HEIGHT:	5'9" to 5'11"	EYES:	Brown
WEIGHT:	160 to 180 lbs	SEX:	Male
		RACE:	Black

CAUTION

Washington Mutual is offering a reward of up to $5,000 to anyone with information leading to the arrest and conviction of the unidentified bank robbery suspect (pictured) in the the Los Angeles area. The suspect is being sought in connection with at least one bank robbery of the American Savings Crenshaw Office located at 3775 Santa Rosalia Drive in Los Angeles. Call We Tip Hotline at 1-800-78-CRIME or the FBI.

WANTED
BANK ROBBERY

** UNIDENTIFIED SUSPECT **
$1,000 REWARD
WANTED BY THE FBI

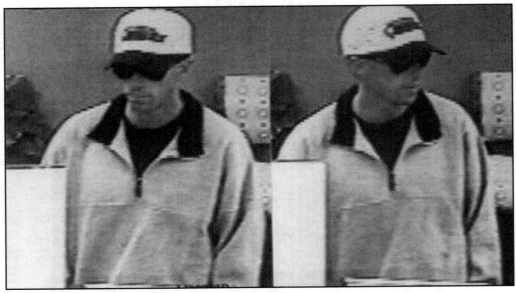

The "Sorry Bandit"
DESCRIPTION

ESTIMATED AGE: 22-28		**HAIR:** Brown, short	
HEIGHT: 5'6" to 5'8"		**EYES:** Unknown	
WEIGHT: 145to 155 lbs		**SEX:** Male	
BUILD: Slender		**RACE:** White	

CLOTHING: The Suspect wears a baseball cap and dark sunglasses, grey pullover sweatshirt with zipper, light color jeans and dark shoes, the suspect always wears Latex Gloves

The "Sorry Bandit" is known to be responsible for the following eleven (11) bank robberies:

02-09-98 – Bay View Federal Daly City, CA
04-14-98 – Western Federal San Bruno, CA
05-01-98 – Downey Savings Redwood City, CA
06-30-98 – California Federal San Mateo, CA
07-27-98 – Washington Mutual Menlo Park, CA
09-09-98 – First National Millbrae, CA

10-27-98 – Washington Mutual Daly City, CA
11-10-98 – Sanwa Bank So. San Francisco, CA
11-10-98 – Home Savings San Francisco, CA
11-24-98 – Home Savings San Francisco, CA
12-22-98 – California Federal Daly City, CA

CAUTION

The "Sorry Bandit" presents the victim teller with a threatening demand note, makes verbal demands for cash, and very often says, "I'm sorry I have to do this to you," before he exits on foot with the cash. Call WeTip Hotline at 1-800-78-CRIME or the FBI.

WANTED
BANK ROBBERY

** UNIDENTIFIED SUSPECT **
$5,000 REWARD
WANTED BY THE FBI

 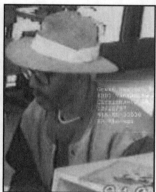  

DESCRIPTION

ESTIMATED AGE:	Mid-30's to early 40's	**HAIR:**	Brown, short
HEIGHT:	6'1"	**EYES:**	Unknown
WEIGHT:	150to 160 lbs	**SEX:**	Male
BUILD:	Slender	**RACE:**	White

The robber has been seen entering a beige mini-van with dark windows and may have a female accomplice described as follows: Race: Black, light complexion. Age: 40's. Height: 5'7". Weight: 130-140 pounds. Hair: Brown, shoulder length.

The suspect is being sought in connection with the following bank robberies:

1/08/98 – Union Bank, 2650 Watt Avenue, Sacramento, CA
12/24/97 – GWB, 8065 Greenback Lane, Sacramento, CA
12/18/97 – Union Bank, 1850 Douglas, Roseville, CA
12/12/97 – GWB, 4001 Manzanita, Carmichael, CA
11/12/97 – GWB, 3600 El Camino, Sacramento, CA
11/08/97 – Cal Fed, 4005 Manzanita, Carmichael, CA

10/09/97 – Union Bank, 2650 Watt Avenue, Sacramento, CA
10/03/97 – B of A, 21 Springtowne Center, Vallejo, CA
09/26/97 – B of A, 2400 N. Texas St, Fairfield, CA
09/10/97 – B of A, 150 Parker St, Vacaville, CA
08/05/97 – American Savings, 5800 Stoneridge Mall,
　　　　　　　Pleasanton, CA

CAUTION
The suspect depicted in the bank surveillance film enters banks, waits in line, then approaches the victim teller. Usually, the robber presents a robbery note, but has also made oral demands. The robber displays a small, silver or chrome colored handgun which he keeps partially hidden in his hands and speaks in a very quiet voice. The robber leaves the area on foot.

WANTED
BANK ROBBERY

✱✱ UNIDENTIFIED SUSPECT ✱✱
$1,000 REWARD
WANTED BY THE FBI

DESCRIPTION

ESTIMATED AGE: 20's	**COMPLEXION:** Pale
HEIGHT: Approximately 6'0"	**SEX:** Male
EYES: Unknown	**RACE:** Caucasion

REMARKS: Suspect was carrying a large day-planner.

CAUTION

SUSPECT INFORMATION: Wanted for robbery of Seattle Metropolitan Branch of Wells Fargo Bank. If you have any information concerning the identity of the above suspect please call the WeTip Hotline at (800) 78-CRIME.

SEEKING INFORMATION

UNKNOWN SUSPECTS

Authorities would like to speak with anyone who may have information concerning the murder or abduction of victims Charles and Jennifer Chia, at or near the Timber Hills apartment complex in Southwest Reno, Nevada on October 18, 1989.

FBI SEEKING INFORMATION

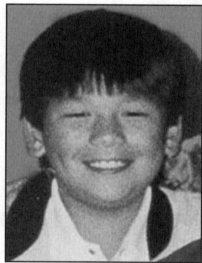
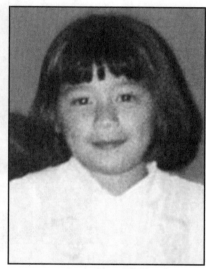

Charles Chia   Jennifer Chia

Victims (Deceased)

THE DETAILS SURROUNDING THE CRIME

At approximately 3:20pm on October 18, 1989, Charles and Jennifer Chia, juveniles, exited their school bus near their residence in the Timber Hills apartment complex in Southwest Reno, Nevada. After exiting the bus they walked across the street with a friend and were last seen walking toward their apartment. Charles Chia, at the time 8 years old with black hair, was wearing a long-sleeve white shirt, a blue pullover, blue jeans and was carrying a dark blue and red backpack. Jennifer Chia, at the time 6 years old with black hair, was wearing a white dress with black dots, white socks, light green shoes and was carrying both a blue tote bag and a "Miss Piggy" lunch pail.

On July 25, 1990 the skeletal remains of Charles and Jennifer Chia were discovered in a shallow grave next to Highway 70 in Plumas County, California, which is approximately 50 miles from Reno, Nevada.

Authorities are also interested in any information that could confirm the possible sighting of Charles and Jennifer Chia in the Northern Nevada area, or in Sierraville or Loyalton, California.

KIDNAPPING

MIRANDA DIANE GADDIS
$50,000 REWARD
FBI MISSING PERSON INVESTIGATION

DESCRIPTION

DATE OF BIRTH:	November 18 1988	**HAIR:**	Blonde
PLACE OF BIRTH:	Unknown	**EYES:**	Brown
HEIGHT:	5'4"	**SEX:**	Female
WEIGHT:	110 lbs	**RACE:**	White

REMARKS: Miranda Gaddis recently dyed her hair blonde. She is known to have a pierced tongue and bellybutton.

Miranda Gaddis was last seen at about 7:30 am on March 8, 2002, in Oregon City, Oregon. Miranda Gaddis was last believed to be wearing a dark blue sweatshirt with the word "Hurley" written on it, blue jeans, and tennis shoes. She was thought to be carrying a dark blue backpack with black netting on the back. The FBI is offering a reward of up to $50,000 for information leading to the arrest of the person(s) responsible for the kidnapping of Miranda Diane Gaddis and Ashley Marie Pond.

KIDNAPPING

ASHLEY MARIE POND
$50,000 REWARD

FBI MISSING PERSON INVESTIGATION

DESCRIPTION

DATE OF BIRTH:	March 1, 1989	**HAIR:**	Brown
PLACE OF BIRTH:	Oregon	**EYES:**	Brown
HEIGHT:	5'3"	**SEX:**	Female
WEIGHT:	110 lbs	**RACE:**	White

REMARKS: Pond has a birthmark on her right hip.

Ashley Marie Pond was last seen leaving her apartment in Oregon City, OR at approximately 8 am on January 9, 2002. The FBI is offering a reward of up to $50,000 for information leading to the arrest of the person(s) responsible for the kidnappings of Ashley Marie Pond and Miranda Diane Gaddis.

KIDNAPPING

KEMBERLY RAMER

$20,000 REWARD

FBI MISSING PERSON INVESTIGATION

DESCRIPTION

DATE OF BIRTH: May 18, 1980	**HAIR:** Brown
HEIGHT: 5'4"	**EYES:** Brown
WEIGHT: 130 lbs	**SEX:** Female
	RACE: White

REMARKS: Ramer has clear braces on her teeth and has thick eyebrows.

Kemberly Ramer disappeared from her residence in Opp, Alabama, on Friday, August 15, 1997. She was last seen leaving a friend's residence to return home, which is about five-minutes away from her friend's home. Ramer lived alone, and after close friends failed to locate her, Ramer's parents reported her disappearance to authorities on Sunday, August 17, 1997.

SEEKING INFORMATION

UNKNOWN SUSPECTS
$100,000 REWARD
FBI SEEKING INFORMATION

These two men are being sought in connection with the abduction of Christina Marie Williams. They are described as being in their early 20's and possibly Asian or from the Pacific Islands.

Victim – Christina Marie Williams

Christina Marie Williams was last seen on the evening of June 12, 1998, at approximately 7:30pm as she departed her home to walk her dog. When her parents found the dog still on its leash near their residence, they phoned the police. The family lives in the Presidio of Monterey Annex area on the former Army Base of Fort Ord near Seaside, California.

A woman, jogging in the vicinity of the area where Christina was last seen, reported to police that on June 12, 1998, she was verbally accosted by two males in a car that had approached her from behind. Later, a second credible witness observed Christina inside the car with the two men. The car is described as an older-model, four-door, light gray with some gray primer paint, Mercury Monarch or Ford Granada with old blue and gold California license plates.

The remains of Christina Williams were found in a wooded field adjacent to the former Fort Ord in Monterey County, California, on January 12, 1999.

If you have any information about this case, you are strongly urged to contact the FBI Command Center at 1-800-671-3343. A reward of up to $100,000 is being offered for any information leading to the identification, arrest, and conviction of the person or persons responsible for the death of Christina Marie Williams.

SEEKING INFORMATION

VICTIMS: WILSON EDISON BLACK ELK, JR. & RONALD OWEN HARD HEART

$20,000 REWARD

FBI SEEKING INFORMATION

Wilson Edison Black Elk, Jr.

Ronald Owen Hard Heart

Victims (Deceased)

THE DETAILS SURROUNDING THE CRIME

On Tuesday, June 8, 1999, the bodies of Wilson Edison Black Elk, Jr. and Ronald Owen Hard Heart were found on the Pine Ridge Indian Reservation(PRIR) in South Dakota, several hundred yards north of the Nebraska-South Dakota border near White Clay, Nebraska. The two victims, both residents of PRIR, were last seen on the main road to Pine Ridge, South Dakota from White Clay, Nebraska on Sunday, June 6, 1999. Authorities have determined that both victims were murdered.

SEEKING INFORMATION
MURDER

VICTIM: SHERRY CAREY

FBI SEEKING INFORMATION

REMARKS: Sherry Carey lived alone. She owned a caricature drawing business and had interest in resale of antique and collectable furniture. She had different groups of friends each associated with different interests. These groups included friends from charity groups, antique furniture sales/restoration, and country western dancing. The night before Carey's death, she went dancing at a country western bar where she met up with several friends. She reportedly left the bar alone as usual.

THE DETAILS SURROUNDING THE CRIME

On October 29, 1992, California Fire Department Officials responded to a report of an explosion at a residence in Long Beach. Upon arrival, fire officials discovered the front door of the residence open and flames coming from the windows. Inside the residence, officials found the body of Sherry Carey lying face down on the bed in one of the rear bedrooms. After the victim was pulled from her home, it was determined that she had been brutally murdered. Her body showed evidence of blunt force trauma, strangulation, and multiple stab wounds. The victim had also been doused with an unknown type of accelerant and set on fire which resulted in first, second and third degree burns across her face and body.

It is believed that the unknown suspect(s) knew Sherry Carey however, authorities are seeking any information regarding this crime.

SEEKING INFORMATION
MURDER

VICTIM: PHILLIP GEORGE COUSINS

$10,500 REWARD

RIVERSIDE, CA POLICE SEEKING INFORMATION

Phillip George Cousins

DESCRIPTION

AGE: 44		**HAIR:** Brown, balding	
HEIGHT: 5'9"		**EYES:** Brown	
WEIGHT: 170 lbs		**SEX:** Male	
		RACE: White	

THE DETAILS SURROUNDING THE CRIME

The Victim was found dead in his Honda Accord in the parking lot of an Industrial complex in the area of First and Sullivan streets in Santa Ana. The victim was last seen on March 3, 1994, at 12:30 p.m. A $10,500 reward given for Information leading to arrest and conviction of person(s) responsible for this murder. Call WeTip Hotline at 1-800 78 CRIME.

INFORMATION WANTED
MURDER INVESTIGATION

** UNIDENTIFIED SUSPECT **
$20,000 REWARD

Orange County Sheriff's Investigators are asking for the public's help in locating the suspects responsible for the shooting death of a Stanton man

WANTED BY STANTON, CA POLICE DEPARTMENT

UNIDENTIFIED SUSPECT

VICTIM: Bernard Garcia Lopez, Jr.

THE DETAILS SURROUNDING THE CRIME

Orange County Sheriff's Investigators are asking for the public's help in locating the suspects responsible for the shooting death of a Stanton man. On Monday, June 30, 1997, at 1:35 a.m., Bernard Garcia Lopez, Jr., 18, (victim photo above right) was with several friends outside his home at 7801 Joel Street, when an unknown suspect came out of the shadows from across the street and began shooting at them. A second suspect remained in the shadows and watched the shooting. Both suspects were last seen running westbound on Joel Street. Suspect #1 (illustration, above left) is described as a Male, Hispanic, 17-21 years old, 5'8" tall, heavy build, head shaved bald, no facial hair, large "jug" type ears, wearing a black sweatshirt, black pants and shoes. Suspect #2 (no composite available) is described as a Male, Hispanic, 20 years old, 5'9" .5'10" tall, 150 lbs., medium length black hair, combed back, no facial hair, wearing a long sleeve black shirt and dark pants. A reward of up to $20,000 is being offered by the City of Stanton and the family and friends of Bernard Garcia Lopez, Jr., for information which leads to the arrest and conviction of the suspects involved in this homicide. If you have information that may help in this case, please call WeTip at (800)78-CRIME.

SEEKING INFORMATION
MURDER

VICTIM: GERALDINE ATHA MYERS
$50,000 REWARD

RIVERSIDE, CA POLICE SEEKING INFORMATION

Geraldine Atha Myers

1983 Toyoya Corolla
4-door, copper color
CA license 1HQC197

Her car was recovered by Las Vegas PD on May 18, 2001

DESCRIPTION

AGE: 81	**HAIR:** Brown
HEIGHT: 5'	**EYES:** Blue
WEIGHT: 97 lbs	**SEX:** Female
	RACE: White

THE DETAILS SURROUNDING THE CRIME

Two separate rewards, totaling $50,000, have been offered by the family and the Riverside County Board of Supervisors for any information directly leading to the capture and conviction of person or persons responsible for the kidnapping and/or murder of Geraldine Atha Myers (Riverside Police Report Number P3-01-135-149) She was last seen at her Riverside residence on Sunday, May 13, 2001 at approximately 8:45pm. Investigators believe foul play was involved in her disappearance.

If you have any information you can call WeTip Anonymously at 800-78-CRIME or you can contact Detective Bill Barnes at (909) 320-8003 or Detective Fred Kelvington at (909) 320-8062 of the Riverside Police department.

SEEKING INFORMATION
MURDER

VICTIM: RICHARD PECK
$25,000 REWARD

**BIG BEAR LAKE, CALIFORNIA DEPUTIES
SEEKING INFORMATION**

THE DETAILS SURROUNDING THE CRIME

Richard Peck, a resident of Big Bear was struck and killed by a HIT-AND-RUN driver on December 17, 2001 at 9:45 PM. James Peck, father of the victim has offered a reward of up to $25,000 for information leading to the arrest of the driver of the car that killed his son

"The parents are personally funding the reward," said Deputy John Emins, of the Victorville Sheriff's Station, who is investigating the case. Peck, who was 19, lived in Big Bear Lake for two years and was employed at Sav-on Drugs. His family resides in the Chino Hills area. It is believed during the evening of Dec. 17, Peck was leaving the Denny's Restaurant located on Big Bear Boulevard at Mountainaire Lane, when he attempted to cross the road about 9:45 p.m. As he stepped out into the boulevard he was struck by what has been described by Sheriff's officials as a dark or black, late-model sedan traveling west.

"The suspect vehicle is believed to have damage near the left headlight," Emins said. "We still do not have the identification of the driver." There was a second vehicle described as an Explorer or Jeep (also dark colored) with a soft top which also stopped but left the scene. Occupants of the second car have committed no crime and are eligible for this reward. Investigators are looking for additional leads right now. Calls can be placed anonymously. We ask that anyone with possible information please phone either of the numbers below.

According to Peck's father, his son was at a party earlier that night. He wasn't sure if his son had been at the restaurant alone or someone had been with him. Emins said he revisited the scene of the accident in a follow-up investigation and did not find any additional information. "I contacted a couple people when I came up, but that went nowhere," Emins said. "We are having a hard time finding anyone who may have seen something. I find that hard to believe, with all those people being at Denny's. We still are talking to anyone who thinks they may have seen anything that night -- no matter how irrelevant they think the information is." If you have any information call WeTip Anonymously at 800-78-CRIME or you can contact The Sheriff's Department at (909) 866-7581 or (909) 866-7582.

SEEKING INFORMATION
MURDER ON INDIAN RESERVATION

VICTIM: DENISE LYNN RUSSELL

$5,000 REWARD

FBI SEEKING INFORMATION

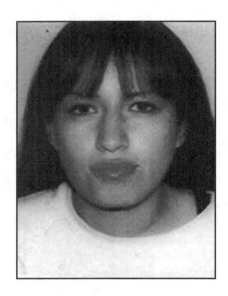

THE DETAILS SURROUNDING THE CRIME

On May 2, 1997, Denise Lynn Russell, an 18-year-old enrolled member of the Northern Cheyenne Tribe, and several friends attended a party at a residence west of Busby, Montana, on the Northern Cheyenne Reservation. After Russell reportedly became upset, she left the party and began walking east on U.S. Highway 212, near Busby, Montana. She was last seen between the hours of 4:00 pm and 5:30 pm.

On September 29, 1997, human remains, later identified as those of Denise Lynn Russell, were found in rural Powder River County, Montana. This area is approximately fifty miles from where Russell was last seen.

U.S. Highway 212 is a two lane road that connects Billings, Montana, with the Black Hills, South Dakota area. The highway also passes through the Crow Indian Reservation and the Northern Cheyenne Reservation. The area around Busby is heavily traveled by semi-trucks and authorities are asking for the public's help in locating anyone who may have seen Ms. Russell along this highway.

SEEKING INFORMATION

VICTIM: TAMMY J. ZYWICKI

FBI SEEKING INFORMATION

DESCRIPTION

DATE OF BIRTH:	March 13, 1971	**HAIR:**	Blonde
HEIGHT:	5'2"	**EYES:**	Green
WEIGHT:	120 lbs	**SEX:**	Female
		RACE:	White

REMARKS: Zywicki was reportedly last seen with her car (shown below) at mile marker 83 in Central Illinois, between 3:10 p.m. and 4:00 p.m. on August 23, 1992. It was also reported that a tractor/trailer was seen near Zywicki's vehicle during this time period. The driver of the tractor/trailer is described as a white male between 35 and 40 years of age, over six feet tall, with dark, bushy hair. Some of the victim's personal property is known to be missing, including a Cannon 35mm camera and a musical wrist watch with the cartoon character "Garfield" on the face.

1985 Pontiac T1000,
New Jersey license plates

THE DETAILS SURROUNDING THE CRIME

On August 23, 1992, Tammy J. Zywicki departed Evanston, Illinois, for college in Grinnell, Iowa, where she was expected to arrive that evening. Later that day, Zywicki's car was found by an Illinois State Trooper and ticketed as being abandoned. On August 24, 1992, the vehicle was towed by the Illinois State Police. On that same evening, Zywicki's mother contacted the Illinois State Police and advised them that her daughter had not arrived at college.

On September 1, 1992, Zywicki's body was located along Interstate Highway 44 (I-44) in rural Lawrence County, Missouri, which is located between Springfield and Joplin, Missouri. She had been stabbed to death.

MISSING PERSON

AMY BRADLEY

REWARD

FBI MISSING PERSON INVESTIGATION

DESCRIPTION

DATE OF BIRTH: May 12, 1974	**HAIR:** Short brown
HEIGHT: 5'6"	**EYES:** Green
WEIGHT: 120 lbs	**SEX:** Female
	RACE: White

REMARKS: Amy Bradley has the following tattoos: a Tasmanian Devil spinning a basketball, on her shoulder; the sun, on her lower back; a Chinese symbol, on her right ankle; and a Gecko lizard, on her navel. She also has a navel ring. A reward is being offered for information leading to Amy Bradley's safe return.

Amy Bradley was reported missing in the early morning hours of March 24, 1998. She was last seen by family members sitting on the balcony outside their cabin aboard the Rhapsody of the Seas cruise ship. The ship was en route to Curacao, Antilles at the time Amy was last seen. The ship docked in Curacao shortly after Amy was discovered missing. Extensive searches on the ship and at sea have produced no signs of Amy's whereabouts. This investigation is ongoing.

Amy Bradley graduated from a college in Virginia with a degree in physical education. She enjoys playing basketball. She would have begun a job working with a computer company upon her return from the trip.

WANTED
TERRORISM SUSPICION

SAID BAHAJI

WANTED BY INTERPOL

DESCRIPTION

DATE OF BIRTH: July 15, 1975	**HAIR:** Black
PLACE OF BIRTH: Haselunne, Germany	**EYES:** Brown
HEIGHT: 6'2"	**RACE:** White
WEIGHT: Unknown	**SEX:** Male
LANGUAGE SPOKEN: German	**NATIONALITY:** German

CAUTION

Offenses: Crimes against public activity/buildings/properties conspiracy, murder conspiracy, terrorism conspiracy, terrorism complicity, terrorism suspicion.

PERSON MAY BE DANGEROUS

FBI LEGAL ATTACHE

The Federal Bureau of Investigation is working every day not only in the United States, but in 52 countries outside our borders. The FBI has a Legal Attache Program which was created to help foster good will and gain greater cooperation with international police partners in support of the FBI's domestic mission. The goal is to link law enforcement resources and other officials outside the U.S. with law enforcement in this country to better ensure the safety of the American public here and abroad.

Presently, there are 44 Legal Attache (Legat) offices and four Legat sub-offices. The FBI's Special Agent representatives abroad carry the titles of Legal Attache, Deputy Legal Attache, or Assistant Legal Attache. The FBI believes it is essential to station highly skilled Special Agents in other countries to help prevent terrorism and crime from reaching across borders and harming Americans in their homes and workplaces.

Legats not only help international police agencies with training activities, they facilitate resolution of the FBI's domestic investigations which have international leads. The Legat program focuses on deterring crime that threatens America such as drug trafficking, international terrorism, and economic espionage.

The FBI's Legal Attache Program is overseen by the International Operations Branch of the Investigative Services Division at FBI Headquarters in Washington, D.C. The International Operations Branch of the FBI keeps in close contact with other federal agencies; Interpol; foreign police and security officers in Washington, D.C.; and national law enforcement associations.

Other international law enforcement organizations:

International Law Enforcement Academy, Budapest, Hungary – 011-36-1-267-4400

Interpol – 011-33-1-4312-2222

Contact the Legal Attache through the American Embassy or Consulate at the following locations:

American Embassy - Almaty, Kazakhstan – 011-7-3272-63-39-21

American Embassy - Amman, Jordan – 011-962-6-592-0101

American Embassy - Ankara, Turkey – 011-90-312-455-5555

American Embassy - Athens, Greece – 011-30-1-721-2951

American Embassy - Bangkok, Thailand – 011-66-2-205-4000

American Embassy - Berlin, Germany – 011-49-30-238-5174

Berlin - Frankfurt Suboffice

American Consulate - Frankfurt, Germany – 011-49-69-7535-0

American Embassy - Bern, Switzerland – 011-41-31-357-7011

American Embassy - Bogota, Colombia – 011-57-1-315-0811

American Embassy - Brasilia, Brazil – 011-55-61-321-7000

American Embassy - Bridgetown, Barbados – 246-436-4950

American Embassy - Brussels, Belgium – 011-32-2-508-2111

American Embassy - Bucharest, Romania – 011-40-1-210-4042

American Embassy - Buenos Aires, Argentina – 011-541-15-777-4533

American Embassy - Cairo, Egypt – 011-202-797-3300

American Embassy - Canberra, Australia – 011-61-2-6214-5600

American Embassy - Caracas, Venezuela – 011-58-212-975-6411

American Embassy - Copenhagen, Denmark – 011-45-3555-3144

American Consulate - Hong Kong, China – 011-852-2523-9011

American Embassy - Islamabad, Pakistan – 011-92-51-2080-0000

American Embassy - Kiev, Ukraine – 011-380-44-490-4000

American Embassy - Lagos, Nigeria – 011-234-1-261-0097

American Embassy - London, England – 011-44-207-499-9000

American Embassy - Madrid, Spain – 011-34-91-587-2200

American Embassy - Manila, Philippines – 011-63-2-523-1001

American Embassy - Mexico City, Mexico – 011-52-5-55080-2000

Mexico City -Guadalajara Suboffice

American Embassy - Mexico City, Mexico – 011-523-33825-2700

Mexico City - Hermosillo

American Embassy - Mexico City, Mexico – 011-526-662217-2375

Mexico City - Monterray Suboffice

American Embassy - Mexico City, Mexico – 011-528-81343-2120

Mexico City - Tijuana

American Embassy - Mexico City, Mexico – 011-526-664681-7400

American Embassy - Moscow, Russia – 011-7-095-728-5000

American Embassy - Nairobi, Kenya 011-254-2-537-800

American Embassy - New Delhi, India – 011-91-11-419-8000

American Embassy - Ottawa, Canada – 1-613-238-5335

Ottawa - Vancouver Suboffice

American Consulate - Vancouver – 1-604-685-4311

American Embassy - Panama City, Panama – 011-507-207-7000

American Embassy - Paris, France – 011-33-1-4312-2222

American Embassy - Prague, Czech Republic 011-420-2-5753-0663

American Embassy - Pretoria, South Africa – 011-27-12-342-1048

American Embassy - Riyadh, Saudi Arabia – 011-966-1-488-3800

American Embassy - Rome, Italy – 011-39-06-4674-2710

American Embassy - Santiago, Chile – 011-56-2-330-5003 (ask for Marines)

American Embassy - Santo Domingo, Dominican Republic 1-809-221-2171

American Embassy - Seoul, South Korea – 011-82-2-397-4114

American Embassy - Singapore, Singapore – 011-65-476-9100

American Embassy - Tallinn, Estonia – 011-372-6-68-8100

American Embassy - Tel Aviv, Israel – 011-972-3-519-7575

American Embassy - Tokyo, Japan – 011-81-3-3224-5000

American Embassy - Vienna, Austria – 011-43-1-313-39-2155

American Embassy - Warsaw, Poland – 011-4822-628-3041

CONTACTS

GOVERNMENT AGENCIES

Air Force Office of Special Investigations
1535 Command Drive
Suite C 309
Andrews AFB, MD 20762-7002
Phone (240) 857-0989
http://www.dtic.mil/afosi/

Bureau of Alcohol Tobacco and Firearms
650 Massachusetts Avenue N.W.
Room 8290
Washington, D.C. 20226
Phone 1-800-ATF-GUNS
http://www.atf.treas.gov

Department of Justice
950 Pennsylvania Avenue N.W.
Washington D.C. 20530-0001
Phone (202) 353-1555
http://www.ibb.gov/

Federal Bureau of Investigation
U.S. Department of Justice
Washington, D.C. 20535
Phone (202) 324-3000
http://www.fbi.gov/

Interpol U.S.
National Central Bureau
Washington D.C. 20530
Phone (202) 616-9000
http://www.interpol.com

Naval Criminal Investigative Service
NCIS Headquarters
Washington, D.C.
Phone 1-800-264-6485
http://www.usdoj.gov.dea

New York City Police Department
Phone 1-800-577-TIPS
http://www.ci.nyc.us/htmlnypd/wanted

Rewards For Justice Program
P.O. Box 96781
Washington, D.C. 20090-6781
Phone 1-800-USREWARDS
http://www.rewardsforjustice.net

Royal Canadian Mounted Police
155 McArthur Avenue
Vanier, Canada
http://rcmp-grc.ca/

U.S. Customs National Law Enforcement Center
1300 Pennsylvania Avenue N.W.
Washington, D.C. 20229
Phone 1-800-BE ALERT
http://www.customs.ustreas.gov

U.S. Drug Enforcement Administration
2401 Jefferson Davis Highway
Alexandria, VA 22301
Phone 1-800-882-9539
http://www.usdoj.gov.dea

U.S. Investigative Support Division
Phone 1-877-CIC-DESK (9242-3375)
http://www.treasury.gov

U.S. Marshals Service
H.Carl Moultrie Courthouse
500 Indiana Avenue N.W.
Washington, D.C. 20001
Phone 1-877-WANTED (926-8332)
http://www.usdoj.gov

U.S. Postal Inspection Services
PO Box 96096
Washington, D.C. 20066-6096
Phone 1-800-654-8896
http://www.usps.com/postalinspectors/

U.S. Secret Service
950 'H' Street N.W.
Washington, D.C. 2223
202-406-5708
http://www.secretservice.gov

PRIVATE AGENCIES

Active Most Wanted and Criminal Investigations
http://www.activemostwanted.com

Alternative Release Bail Bond Service
Phone 1-800-669-2245
http://www.mostwanted.org

CASE BREAKERS.COM
http://www.rewardsclearinghouse.com

Felony Finders
http://www.felonyfinders.com

The World's Most Wanted, Inc.
12600 Morrow Avenue, NE. Suite A1
Albuquerque, NM 8712-4735
http://www.mostwanted.org

We Tip Crime Net
Phone 1-800-78-CRIME
http://www.wetip.com

Wells Fargo
Phone 1-800-78-CRIME
http://www.wellsfargo.com/wanted

INDEX

INDEX